UNIVERSITIES AND ECONOMIC DEVELOPMENT IN AFRICA

Nico Cloete, Tracy Bailey, Pundy Pillay, Ian Bunting and Peter Maassen

HERANA   CHET

Published by the Centre for Higher Education Transformation (CHET),
House Vincent, First Floor, 10 Brodie Road, Wynberg Mews, Wynberg, 7800
Telephone: +27(0)21 763-7100 | Fax: +27(0)21 763-7117
E-mail: chet@chet.org.za | www.chet.org.za

© CHET 2011

ISBN 978-1-920355-73-9

Produced by COMPRESS.dsl | www.compressdsl.com

Cover illustration by Raymond Oberholzer

Distributed by African Minds
4 Eccleston Place, Somerset West, 7130, South Africa
info@africanminds.co.za
www.africanminds.co.za

For orders from outside Africa:
African Books Collective
PO Box 721, Oxford OX1 9EN, UK
orders@africanbookscollective.com
www.africanbookscollective.com

Contents

Tables, figures and boxes

Tables

Figures

Boxes

Acknowledgements

During the post-independence period, every African country has struggled with the vexing issue of the role of higher education in development. While many studies on higher education in Africa deal with this problematic indirectly, very few have actually taken it on directly. It took a consultation and discussion period of almost three years between the Centre for Higher Education Transformation (CHET), senior researchers and the US Partnership for Higher Education in Africa to establish the Higher Education Research and Advocacy Network in Africa (HERANA).[1]

Credit must be given to the US Partnership for supporting such a complex and potentially controversial project – and one which would not easily have been funded by a single foundation. Having on board the Ford Foundation, the Carnegie Corporation of New York, the Rockefeller Foundation and the Kresge Foundation contributed to the credibility of the project amongst higher education leaders and academics. A special word of thanks must go to Dr John Butler-Adam (Ford), who 'steered' the Partnership in this project, and to Dr Claudia Frittelli (Carnegie), who participated actively throughout.

The capacity-building component of HERANA is the Higher Education Masters in Africa, run jointly between the universities of the Western Cape, Makerere and Oslo, with students from eight African countries. The Masters programme is funded by the NOMA programme of the Norwegian Agency for Development Cooperation (NORAD) with Ms Tove Kivil a constant source of support.

We must also acknowledge the vice-chancellors of the eight participating universities who expressed their confidence in the project and identified relevant staff (see Project Group below) to provide institutional data and participate in the network. The full list of project participants is included in Appendix B.

A special word of thanks must also go to Professor Manuel Castells, whose seminal 1991 paper, *The University System: Engine of development in the new world economy*, not only shifted the thinking of agencies such as the World Bank, but was an inspiration to the project group. Prof. Castells' continued participation and support is both a motivation and a challenge.

We must acknowledge the fortuitous coincidence of HERANA and *University World News* starting at almost the same time. *University World News*, with its 30 000 readers, around 14 000 of whom subscribe to the Africa edition, has been a source of information for our

---

1   For a description of the various HERANA project components, participants and publications, visit the website at http://www.chet.org.za/programmes/herana/.

project and a distribution resource. It has been a pleasure being in partnership with the editor, Karen MacGregor.

Finally, our thanks go to the Board of CHET, which not only expressed confidence in the CHET leadership, but participated in consultations to establish HERANA. Four members who participated actively in the project are Prof. Teboho Moja (Chair of the Board, New York University), Dr Lidia Brito (UNESCO), Dr Goolam Mohamedbhai (former Secretary-General, Association of African Universities), and Dr Esi Sutherland-Addy (University of Ghana).

The project group

Academic advisers	*Higher Education Studies*: Prof. Peter Maassen (University of Oslo) and Dr Nico Cloete (Director: CHET, and University of the Western Cape)
	Development Economics: Prof. Pundy Pillay (University of the Witwatersrand)
	Sociology of Knowledge: Prof. Johan Muller (University of Cape Town)
Researchers	Dr Nico Cloete (Director: CHET)
	Dr Pundy Pillay (University of the Witwatersrand)
	Prof. Peter Maassen (University of Oslo)
	Ms Tracy Bailey (CHET Project Manager)
	Dr Gerald Ouma (University of the Western Cape)
	Mr Romulo Pinheiro (University of Oslo)
	Dr Patricio Langa (Eduardo Mondlane University and University of the Western Cape)
Academic core data and analysis	Dr Ian Bunting (Department of Education and CHET Consultant) and Dr Charles Sheppard (Nelson Mandela Metropolitan University) collected and analysed the academic core data
	Mr Nelius Boshoff (Centre for Research on Science and Technology, University of Stellenbosch) collected data on research output
Project assistance	Ms Angela Mias (CHET Administrator)
	Ms Karen MacGregor, Ms Stefanie Swanepoel and Ms Michelle Willmers (Editing)
	Ms Monique Ritter (Research assistance and data checking)
	Ms Carin Favis (Transcription)
	Ms Kathy Graham and Ms Marlene Titus (Funds management)

External Commentators

Prof. Manuel Castells (University of Southern California, Los Angeles, and Internet Interdisciplinary Institute, Open University Catalonia, Barcelona)

Prof. John Douglass (Centre for Studies in Higher Education, University of California, Berkeley)

University contacts

Botswana: Prof. Isaac Mazonde (Director, Research and Development), Mr David Katzke (Deputy Vice-chancellor, Finance and Administration), Mr Silas Onalenna (Assistant Director, Institutional Research)

Dar es Salaam: Prof. Daniel Mkude (Department of Linguistics), Prof. Amandina Lihamba (Acting Director, Directorate of Public Service)

Eduardo Mondlane: Prof. Maria da Conceição and Dr Patricio Langa (Faculty of Education)

Ghana: Prof. Ben Ahunu (Provost, College of Agriculture and Consumer Sciences), Mr Alfred Quartey (Director, Planning), Dr Joseph Budu (Registrar)

Makerere: Prof. Vincent Ssembatya (Director, Quality Assurance), Dr Florence Nakayiwa-Mayega (Department of Planning and Development)

Mauritius: Prof. Kishore Baguant (Director, Quality Assurance), Prof. Henri Li kam Wah (Faculty of Science), Ms Anjana Daiboo (Office for Quality Assurance)

Nairobi: Mr Bernard Waweru (Registrar), Mr Samuel Kiiru (Institute for Development Studies)

Nelson Mandela Metropolitan: Prof. Heather Nel (Director, Strategic and Institutional Planning), Dr Charles Sheppard (Director, Management Information)

Acronyms and abbreviations

CHET	Centre for Higher Education Transformation
FTE	Full-time equivalent
GDP	Gross domestic product
HDI	Human Development Index
HERANA	Higher Education Research and Advocacy Network in Africa
ISI	Institute for Scientific Information
NGO	Non-governmental organisation
NMMU	Nelson Mandela Metropolitan University
OECD	Organisation for Economic Cooperation and Development
PPP	Purchasing power parity
R&D	Research and development
SACMEQ	Southern and Eastern Africa Consortium for Monitoring Educational Quality
SET	Science, engineering and technology
SIDA/SAREC	Swedish International Development Cooperation Agency/Department of Research Cooperation
SME	Small and medium enterprise
UNDP	United Nations Development Programme
UNESCO	United Nations Educational, Scientific and Cultural Organisation
US	United States of America
USD	United States Dollar
WEF	World Economic Forum

PART 1
INTRODUCTION
AND BACKGROUND TO THE STUDY

We begin in this section with a brief overview of trends in the relationship between higher education and development both internationally and in the African context. We then introduce the focus, methodology and analytical points of departure for the current study.

1.1　The relationship between higher education and development[2]

International trends

Over the past couple of decades, 'globalisation' and the emergence of the 'knowledge economy' have given rise to new economic, social, political and cultural challenges to which nations, regions and higher education systems and institutions are responding. It is widely assumed that in the context of these new challenges specific knowledge, competencies and skills – often referred to as 'human capital' – come to play an increasingly important role in developmental efforts, as do research, innovation and technological development (Castells 2002). Knowledge production, accumulation, transfer and application have become major factors in socio-economic development and are increasingly at the core of national development strategies for gaining competitive advantages in the global knowledge economy (Santiago *et al.* 2008; World Bank 1999, 2002).

Higher education institutions are seen by many as playing a key role in delivering the knowledge requirements for development. Research has, for example, suggested a strong association between higher education participation rates and levels of development. While the higher education participation rates in many high-income countries are well over 50%, in sub-Saharan Africa they are in most cases below 5% (Bloom *et al.* 2006). Furthermore, there is increasing evidence that high levels of education in general, and of higher education in particular, are essential for the design and productive use of new technologies, while they also provide the foundations for a nation's innovative capacity, and contribute more than any other social institution to the development of civil society (Carnoy *et al.* 1993; Serageldin 2000).

This type of 'evidence' has led to a number of countries putting knowledge and innovation policies, as well as higher education, at the core of their development strategies. The best known model in a developed country is that of Finland which, following the deep recession of the early 1990s, selected knowledge, information technology and education as the major cornerstones of the new (economic) development policy (Hölttä & Malkki 2000). South Korea, Singapore, Denmark, Australia and New Zealand have also followed this route successfully.

The Chinese and Indian economies have displayed unprecedented levels of sustained growth since the early 1990s. China embarked on a knowledge-based growth track by attracting massive foreign direct investment and then building indigenous knowledge capacity through huge investments in education and research. India has succeeded by making the best use of its elite education institutions and exploiting international information technology-related opportunities, in part through the deft use of knowledge assets. The Chinese and Indian economies, however, exhibit two important characteristics with respect to higher education that set them apart from both the 'East Asian tigers' of the 1980s and from some other contemporary developing countries. First, investment in higher education is seen as a parallel process (and not a consecutive one) to providing broader access to and improving the quality of primary and secondary schooling. The second, related, point illustrated in the development pattern of the Chinese and Indian economies is that the traditional growth path of domination first of primary sector activities (agriculture and mining) followed by manufacturing and then by services, does not necessarily hold.

The speed and extent to which developing countries are able to absorb, utilise and modify technology developed mainly in high-income countries, will determine whether they will be able to realise a more rapid transition to higher levels of development and standards of living. In this way, some developing countries and emerging economies have 'leap-frogged' stages of development by investing in higher education.

The African context

What has been the link between higher education and economic development in Africa?

The history and specifics of the African context have given rise to particular interpretations of the role of higher education in national development. Following independence, universities in Africa[3] were expected to be key contributors to the human resource needs of the countries in which they were located. There was a particular focus on the development of human resources for the civil service and the public professions. This was to address the acute shortages in these areas that were the result of the gross underdevelopment of universities under colonialism, and the departure of colonial administrators and professionals following independence.

The year 1960 was heralded in many international circles as the 'Year of Africa' and the beginning of the so-called 'development decade'. In September 1962, UNESCO hosted a conference on the Development of Higher Education in Africa. A decade later, in July 1972, the Association of African Universities held a workshop in Accra which focused on 'the role of the university in development' (Yesufu 1973). The importance of the university in newly-independent African countries was underscored by the now-famous 'Accra declaration' that all universities must be 'development universities' (ibid.). Controversially, workshop participants agreed that this was such an important task that the university could not be left to academics alone; it was also the responsibility of governments to steer universities in the development direction.[4]

While many nationalist African academics enthusiastically supported the role of the 'development university', seeing it as a plus in their contestations with the expatriate professoriate that dominated institutions, it sat uncomfortably with expatriates and some 'worldly' African academics. This latter group was more comfortable with the traditional model of the university as a self-governing institution (i.e. governed primarily by scholars) that predominated in the UK and the US at the time. This self-governing model was the

---

3   At the time of independence, the higher education systems in most African countries were limited to a single national university. It is thus not possible to speak of a higher education system as such at that time.

4   Arguably, this was the last time, until 2009, that governments in Africa agreed, at least in continental statements, that universities are important for development (MacGregor 2009a).

dominant model during the first two decades following independence and there was strong agreement between universities and 'liberation' governments[5] that the role of elite universities was to produce human capital for the new state.

Despite the rhetoric about the 'development university', African governments did little to promote the development role of universities. In part this was because many of these governments had not developed a coherent development model. In addition, many had become increasingly embroiled in internal power struggles, and the external politics of the Cold War and funding agencies such as the World Bank. Instead, 'not leaving the universities alone' became interference by government, rather than steering (Moja *et al.* 1996). In turn, universities became sites of contestation – partially around the development model of the new state, and partially around lack of delivery, which included inadequate funding for the institutions. The result was that many governments, other stakeholders and academics became sceptical, if not suspicious, of the university's role in national development. This led to a notion that higher education was a 'luxury ancillary'[6] – nice to have, but not necessary – in part, because it was difficult to see what contribution universities were making to development; in part, because of prolonged economic crises and the high costs associated with higher education.

It was during this period that the World Bank, in particular, based on the infamous 'rate of return to investments in education' study (Psacharopoulos *et al.* 1986), concluded that development efforts in Africa should be refocused to concentrate on primary education. This is clearly evident in the dramatic decreases in per capita spending on higher education in Africa: 'Public expenditure per tertiary student has fallen from USD 6 800 in 1980, to USD 1 200 in 2002, and recently averaged just USD 981 in 33 low-income SSA [sub-Saharan Africa] countries' (World Bank 2009: xxvii). This is a staggering decrease of 82%.

Unlike the approach in China and India of emphasising higher education and primary and secondary education simultaneously in their development strategies, the World Bank strategy in Africa had the effect of delinking universities from development. In addition, it led to development policies that had negative consequences for African nations and their sustainable development potential. Neglect of higher education led to the disestablishment of research centres, medical schools, agricultural centres, telecommunication and technological development, business training centres, vocational schools and other areas in the higher education sector, which are critical to the development of African societies and their economies.[7]

During the 1990s and early 2000s, some influential voices started calling for the revitalisation of the African university and for linking higher education to development (Sawyerr 2004). The World Bank itself, influenced by Castells' (1991) path-breaking paper, *The University System: Engine of development in the new world economy*, started embracing the role of higher education in the knowledge economy, and for development

---

5   Many of the liberation leaders had studied at foreign universities.

6   World Bank specialists suggested at a meeting with African university vice-chancellors in 1986 that higher education in Africa was a luxury; that it might be better to close some institutions, or send those needing graduate work abroad (Brock-Utne 2003: 30).

7   The decline and the commercialisation of African universities has been well documented and need not be elaborated here. See, for example, Mamdani (2008) and Fred Hayward's contribution to the US Congress Sub-committee on African Affairs (US Congress 1994).

in the developing world (World Bank 2002). This has subsequently been strengthened by World Bank-sponsored studies such as Bloom *et al.* (2006) which empirically demonstrated a relationship between investment in higher education and gross domestic product in Africa. Additional evidence has been generated by subsequent studies by the African Development Bank (Kamara & Nyende 2007) and the World Bank (2009).

Kofi Annan, then secretary general of the United Nations, strongly promoted the importance of universities for development in Africa (quoted in Bloom *et al.* 2006: 2):

> *The university must become a primary tool for Africa's development in the new century. Universities can help develop African expertise; they can enhance the analysis of African problems; strengthen domestic institutions; serve as a model environment for the practice of good governance, conflict resolution and respect for human rights, and enable African academics to play an active part in the global community of scholars.*

This rather ambitious claim for higher education was endorsed by a group of African ministers of education at a preparatory meeting for the UNESCO World Conference on Higher Education in 2009. MacGregor (2009b) reported that the ministers 'called for improved financing of universities and a support fund to strengthen training and research in key areas'.

While the above statements clearly demonstrate support for the role of higher education in development, they do little to clarify what this role is. There seem to be two different notions hidden within the idea of a 'development tool' – a direct, instrumentalist or 'service' role, and an 'engine of development' role which is based on strengthening knowledge production and the role of universities in innovation processes.

The instrumentalist role is arguably the most dominant of the two notions in Africa. For instance, the demands by, especially, foreign donors and multilateral agencies such as the United Nations and UNESCO for university revitalisation are, in many cases, underpinned by the assumption that universities are 'repositories of expertise' which should be applied to solving pressing development issues, such as poverty reduction and education for all.

This thinking of 'university as service provider' in Africa is also strongly present within academia itself, and particularly in certain post-colonial contexts. *University World News* reported that at the Association of Commonwealth Universities conference (April 2010) it was stated that: 'Universities must be "citadels not silos", defending communities around them rather than being inward-looking, if they are to actively advance global development goals' (MacGregor & Makoni 2010), and that universities must 'orientate their activities more directly towards supporting UN Millennium Development Goals' (MacGregor 2010). The chief executive officer of the Southern African Regional Universities Association, Piyushi Kotecha, argued that in recent decades, higher education had assumed growing importance for both personal development and for driving social and economic development: 'Now more than ever before, higher education in developing nations is being expected to take on the mantle of responsibility for growth and development, where often governments fail' (ibid.).

This 'direct' instrumentalist notion assumes that universities have a concentration (surplus) of expertise, and presumably spare time, that must be applied directly, or in partnership, to pressing socio-economic issues, such as poverty, disease, governance and the competitiveness of private firms or companies.

The second role for higher education embedded in Annan's 'development tool' is Castells' 'engine of development' notion, which has become the dominant discourse for many advanced OECD (Organisation for Economic Cooperation and Development) countries. Castells (2009) described this notion as follows:

> *In the current condition of the global knowledge economy, knowledge production and technological innovation become the most important productive forces. So, without at least some level of a national research system, which is composed of universities, the private sector, public research centres and external funding, no country, even the smallest country, can really participate in the global knowledge economy.*

There have, more recently, been calls for this kind of engagement of higher education in development. For example, the high-profile African scientist at Harvard, Calestous Juma, has consistently promoted the role of higher education in science-led development through, amongst others, the UN Millennium Project Task Force on Science, Technology and Innovation (Juma & Yee-Cheong 2005). In addition, the African Ministerial Council on Science and Technology (AMCOST), established in November 2003 under the auspices of the New Partnership for Africa's Development (NEPAD) and the African Union, created a high-level platform for developing policies and setting priorities on science, technology, research and innovation for development in Africa.

1.2   The focus of prior research

As Pillay's (2010a) review of the literature shows, much of the research that has been undertaken on the relationship between higher education and economic development has been econometric in nature. Examples of such studies include the following:

- Impact of higher education on economic growth, for example studies that measure the correlation between higher education participation rates (i.e. the proportion of the population with higher education qualifications) and economic growth rate or technological advance – globally, regionally or locally.
- 'Rates of return' studies which measure the private and public benefits of investing in higher education (e.g. increased tax revenues, saving and investments, or a more productive, entrepreneurial and civic society).
- The role of higher education in producing human capital for the labour market (e.g. issues relating to scarce skills, shortage/oversupply of skills and individual mobility).

- Studies that focus on how higher education institutions can contribute to the capabilities of private firms to take up new technologies, including the growing importance of university–industry linkages.
- The implications of the knowledge economy for higher education institutions in terms of the kinds of graduates that are required (e.g. lifelong learning, preparation for knowledge-intensive jobs , etc.) and the way in which research is undertaken, as well as implications for the policy and regulatory framework within which these institutions operate.

While, broadly speaking, the body of literature on higher education and economic development has grown considerably over the past couple of decades, there are still a number of limitations to the prior research conducted in this area. For instance, little work has been done which focuses on the characteristics and dynamics of the relationship between higher education and development, or on the contextual and institutional factors which facilitate or inhibit these relationships. Neither has there been much research within the African context, or that takes both national and institutional factors into account.

This study attempted to address these gaps and to do so from theoretical perspectives offered by the fields of higher education studies, institutional theory and development economics. This implies that in developing our analytical model we did not want to follow the 'African exceptionalism' approach.[8] In our view, for understanding the contributions of African universities to (economic) development, we first and foremost had to examine these institutions as universities, taking the unique, basic characteristics of universities as a starting point (see, for example, Clark 1983). In addition, for developing a valid analytical framework we also incorporated relevant conceptualisations from the general social sciences. As a consequence, the analytical point of departure for our model was that the conditions under which each university in Africa, as elsewhere, is contributing to economic development are influenced by the following three inter-related factors:

1. The nature of the pact between universities, political authorities and society at large;
2. The nature, strength, size, quality and continuity of the university's academic core; and
3. The level of coordination, effectiveness of implementation, and connectedness in the larger policy context of universities.

These, in turn, are influenced by local circumstances, for example, the nature of the economy of a country, and its political and governance traditions and culture; institutional characteristics, including the 'loosely-coupled' nature of higher education institutions; and the external relations of universities, especially with national authorities, foreign agencies and industry.

---

8   See, for example, Altbach and Balán (2007), who, in their book *World Class Worldwide*, focused on the transformations of research universities in Asia and Latin America. They did not include Africa because they believed 'that Africa's academic challenges are sufficiently different from those of the nations represented here that comparison would not be appropriate' (Altbach & Balán 2007: vii). Strikingly, the authors did not provide any arguments or data to support their claims.

1.3   Project process and methodology

As a point of departure, the overall aim of the study was to investigate the complex relationships between higher education (specifically universities) and economic development in selected African countries with a focus on the context in which universities operate (political and socio-economic), the internal structure and dynamics of the universities themselves, and the interaction between the national and institutional contexts. In addition, the study aimed to identify those factors (practices, strategies) and conditions (context) – at both national and institutional levels – that facilitate or inhibit universities' ability to make a sustainable contribution to economic development.

The project began with a review of the international literature on the relationship between higher education and economic development (Pillay 2010a). This was followed by case studies of three systems which have successfully linked their economic development and higher education policy and planning – Finland, South Korea and North Carolina state in the US (Pillay 2010b).

The next phase of the project involved the collection of data at both the national and institutional levels in the eight African countries and universities included in the study. These were:

- Botswana and the University of Botswana
- Ghana and the University of Ghana
- Kenya and the University of Nairobi
- Mauritius and the University of Mauritius
- Mozambique and the Eduardo Mondlane University
- South Africa and the Nelson Mandela Metropolitan University
- Tanzania and the University of Dar es Salaam, and
- Uganda and Makerere University.

The countries included in the study were selected primarily on the basis of previous collaboration, and on the basis of World Economic Forum (WEF) ratings regarding location in the knowledge economy 'rankings'. The WEF's rating classifies the eight African countries and the three international case study countries according to their 'stage of development' as either factor-, efficiency- or innovation-driven.

In the 'first stage of development', the economy is 'factor-driven' and countries compete based on their factor endowments: primarily unskilled labour and natural resources. As wages rise with advancing development, countries move into the 'efficiency-driven' stage of development, when they must begin to develop more efficient production processes and increase product quality. At this point competitiveness is increasingly driven by higher education and training, amongst other things. Finally, as countries move into the 'innovation-driven' stage, they compete through producing new and different goods by combining sophisticated production processes with a high-skill workforce, research and innovation.

The three 'successful' systems – Finland, South Korea and the US (North Carolina) – are classified as innovation-driven; South Africa and Mauritius are classified as efficiency-driven; Botswana is moving from factor-driven to efficiency-driven; and the remaining five countries are at the factor-driven stage. (See Appendix A for a higher education and development profile of the countries included in the study.)

In each of the collaborating countries the national ('flagship') university was selected, except in South Africa where Nelson Mandela Metropolitan University (NMMU) was regarded as a more 'comparable' institution in terms of size and profile. For the analysis of the academic core, we also included the University of Cape Town, which is the number-one-ranked university in Africa, both in the Times Higher Education World University Rankings and the Shanghai rankings.

The research team visited the eight African countries and universities between February and June 2009. Semi-structured interviews were conducted with a wide range of individuals in each country, including central actors in selected ministries and commissions/councils for higher education and other stakeholders at the national level; and in universities, institutional leadership, senior academics, administrators and project leaders. (See Appendix B for the list of interviewees.) The interviews with institutional stakeholders were transcribed, enabling direct quotation in the case study reports. Transcription of the national stakeholder interviews was not always possible as in some cases these were not recorded owing to government 'sensitivities'.

The analysis also drew on various policy and strategy documents (national and institutional levels), as well as quantitative data including national development indicators and statistics relating to the higher education systems and universities in the sample.

In addition to the literature review (Pillay 2010a) and the case studies of successful systems (Pillay 2010b), the primary outputs of this study include detailed case study reports of the eight African countries and universities included in the sample,[9] and a synthesis report[10] which pulls together the key findings of the study.

Throughout the project process, various efforts were made to engage with the national and institutional stakeholders in each of the eight African countries that participated in the project, in order to obtain feedback regarding the accuracy and completeness of data collection, as well as the interpretation of the data:

- During 2009 and 2010, work-in-progress was presented via seminars to stakeholders in six of the African countries, and to academics in the field such as at the Consortium of Higher Education Researchers (CHER) conference (Oslo 2010) and the University of the Western Cape seminar with Manuel Castells (Cape Town 2009).
- In the drafting of the case study reports, additional information as well as clarification was obtained from national and institutional stakeholders via email. The information

---

9   The eight African case study reports can be accessed at http://www.chet.org.za/programmes/herana/.
10   The synthesis report and the executive summary of the synthesis report are available at http://www.chet.org.za/books/universities-and-economic-development-africa.

gathered on the development projects was compiled in table form and emailed to the respective project leaders with a request to check for accuracy and to fill in any gaps.

- In August 2010, the draft case study reports were emailed to the vice-chancellor and one or two other institutional leaders, as well as the project leaders, in each of the eight universities to request their feedback. A two-day seminar[11] was held in South Africa that month, attended by at least two representatives from each country, during which detailed feedback was obtained on the reports.

Finally, a feature of this study is that the core concepts of 'pact', 'academic core', 'coordination' and 'connectedness' were operationalised through, amongst other things, the use of specific indicators, which allowed us to gather comparable empirical evidence. Throughout the project process, team members met to discuss their ratings and interpretations of the research findings as these were emerging and to further develop the analytical framework for the study.

A note about the data timeframe

It should be noted that the data on which this study is based range from 2001–2009. In particular, the academic core data cover the period 2001–2007, while the national and institutional policies, plans and project information is based on data collected in 2009.

1.4 Analytical starting points for the study

In the knowledge economy, universities are considered to be key institutions for the production of high-level skills and knowledge of relevance for private and public sector innovation processes, based on the traditional core business of universities – the production, application and dissemination of knowledge.

In many countries, higher education has become one of the central areas in the government's knowledge policies. This means that more policy/political actors than the ministry of education, as well as socio-economic stakeholders (employers' organisations, funders and research councils), have become interested in higher education and involved in higher education policy. As a consequence, system- and institutional-level coordination of knowledge policies with adequate structures and processes within the political system have become major issues, most notably the capacity to coordinate different political activities of the governing of knowledge production, reproduction and coordination.

As mentioned earlier, to get a better understanding of the relationship between higher education and development, the research group undertook case studies of systems where there is a well-established integration of higher education in national development strategies. The three case studies are Finland, South Korea and the state of North Carolina in the US – all three located in OECD member countries on different continents. One of the main reasons for choosing these three was that in all cases there was evidence of a strong

---

11   For more information about this seminar, visit the CHET website: http://www.chet.org.za/higher-education-and-economic-development-africa-report-back-herana.

and close relationship between education and economic development in general, and higher education and economic development in particular. In addition, in all three systems a rethink of major economic policies was accompanied by a deliberate attempt to link higher education to economic development.

Of particular interest to our study was the question: What is it about these three systems that enable them to successfully link higher education to economic development? Put another way: What are the core conditions that are present in each of the three systems that enable their higher education sectors to successfully and sustainably contribute to development?

Common to all three systems was a strong, agreed-upon development framework aimed at realising an advanced, competitive knowledge economy, and an important role for higher education in this regard. Despite major contextual differences, the three systems exhibited the following conditions for harnessing higher education for economic development:

- Their higher education systems had been built on a foundation of equitable and quality schooling. There was also an emphasis on achieving high quality higher education.
- They had achieved very high participation rates in higher education (see Appendix A).
- Their higher education systems were differentiated (institutional and public/private) as part of achieving their human capital, research and innovation objectives for economic development.
- Their governments ensured a close link between economic and (higher) education planning.
- There were effective partnerships and networks between the state, higher education institutions and the private sector to ensure effective education and training, and to stimulate appropriate research and innovation.
- There was strong state involvement in a number of other respects including, for example, adequate state funding for higher education; using funding to steer the higher education sector to respond to labour market requirements; and incentivising research and innovation in the higher education sector.

Drawing on the review of the literature (Pillay 2010a), the implications from the case studies of three successful systems (Pillay 2010b), and preliminary observations from the eight African case studies, we formulated the following analytical propositions:

- A condition for effective university contributions to development is the existence of a broad pact between government, universities and core socio-economic actors about the nature of the role of universities in development.
- As a core knowledge institution, the university can only participate in the global knowledge economy and make a sustainable contribution to development if its academic core is quantitatively and qualitatively strong.
- For linking universities effectively to development a country needs various forms and methods of knowledge policy coordination. In addition, the connectedness between the larger policy context, universities and development is crucial.

These analytical propositions provided a three-prong focus for the analysis of the data, namely: the existence of a pact on the role of universities in economic development; the nature and the strength of the academic core of the universities; and the extent of knowledge policy coordination and the connections between key stakeholders.

What the study did not do

As can been seen from the outline above, this study had a considerable scope. Nevertheless, the project did not attempt to:

- Measure or evaluate the extent to which universities were contributing to development, or the impact that their activities had on development in their respective countries.
- Assess the impact or effectiveness of specific institutional policies, units or development projects.
- Review the number or nature of donor projects, or examine the overall contribution of particular external donors to university development.
- Assume or assert that the primary role for higher education is development, but rather sought to investigate the factors that either facilitate or inhibit the possible contributions that universities can make to development.

1.5 The structure of this book

Part 2 presents a synthesis of the key findings of the eight African case studies, organised around the three components of the conceptual framework, namely, the nature and extent of a pact on higher education's role in development; the nature and strength of the academic cores of the eight universities in the sample; and coordination and connectedness that link universities to development.

Part 3 provides the key findings of each of the eight case studies. This includes a brief overview of the higher education and economic development contexts within each country; the extent to which there was evidence of a pact around the role of the university in development; the extent to which knowledge policies and activities were coordinated in each country; a rating of the strength of the academic cores of the eight universities in the sample; and an assessment of the connectedness of each university to its external stakeholders and its academic core.

Part 4 draws out the main conclusions of the study, as well as the implications for further research and action, with regard to the three conceptual points of departure. These include the need for a pact on a role for the university as an 'engine for development'; the need to strengthen the academic cores of African universities via, amongst others, improving incentive structures; and the need to improve policy and implementation coordination at national and institutional levels in order to connect universities more effectively to development.

Part 2
SYNTHESIS OF THE KEY FINDINGS

The analytical point of departure for this study was that the conditions under which universities in Africa, as elsewhere, are contributing to economic development are influenced by the following three inter-related factors:

- The nature of the pact between universities, political authorities and society at large;
- The nature, strength, size, quality and continuity of the university's academic core; and
- The level of coordination, effectiveness of implementation, and connectedness in the larger policy context of universities.

In this section, we present a synthesis of the key findings in the eight African case studies. We begin by exploring the extent to which there was a pact among national and university stakeholders about the role of higher education in development. We then consider the nature and strength of the academic core of the eight African universities in the sample. We conclude by discussing the findings on the extent to which there was coordination at the national level with regard to universities' role in development, and whether the development activities of the universities served to strengthen their academic core.

2
Universities and economic development: Evidence of a pact?

For the purposes of this study, we used the definition of a pact provided by Gornitzka *et al.* (2007: 184):

> A 'pact' is a fairly long-term cultural commitment to and from the university, as an institution with its own foundational rules of appropriate practices, causal and normative beliefs, and resources, yet validated by the political and social system in which the university is embedded. A pact, then, is different from a contract based on continuous strategic calculation of expected value by public authorities, organised external groups, university employees, and students – all regularly monitoring and assessing the university on the basis of its usefulness for their self-interest, and acting accordingly.

The key actors of the pact are national, institutional and external stakeholders. It is assumed that the stronger the pact between universities, university leadership, national authorities and society at large, the better the universities will be able to make a significant, sustainable contribution to development.

Our interest was in exploring the extent to which there was a pact around the role for higher education in society in general and in economic development in particular in each of the eight African countries. Key to the development of such a pact is agreement or consensus that there should be a role for higher education and then about what that role should entail. In order to investigate this aspect, we sought to address the following questions:

1. Is there a role for knowledge production and for universities in the national development plan?
2. How do the relevant national authorities and institutional stakeholders talk about and conceptualise the role of universities, and is there consensus or disjuncture?

In order to investigate these various dimensions of the pact, we collected and analysed an array of both documentary and interview data. At the national level, we consulted national vision documents as well as policies, plans and/or strategies for development, higher education, and science and technology. Interviews were conducted with a range of national stakeholders, such as representatives of the ministries responsible for higher education, finance or economic affairs, and science and technology, as well as representatives from tertiary/higher education councils/commissions. At the university level, we examined key institutional documents such as the strategic plan and the research policy. We conducted interviews with university leaders, including the vice-chancellor and/or deputy vice-chancellors, heads of research and institutional planning, deans of faculties and directors of centres, and other senior academics.

2.1 The role of knowledge and universities in development

A role for knowledge and universities in national and institutional policies and plans

From the interviews and policy documents it was evident that none of the eight African countries included in the study had a clearly articulated development model or strategy. Some countries had national development plans (e.g. Uganda, Botswana and Mozambique), others had poverty reduction strategies (e.g. Ghana and Mozambique), and a number of countries had national visions – usually focused far away in time (e.g. *Tanzania Development Vision 2025*, *Botswana Vision 2016*, *Ghana Vision 2020*, *Mozambique's Agenda 2025*, *Kenya Vision 2030*). However, these did not constitute development models and were often based on 'best practice' policy-borrowing from first world countries. Mauritius came the closest to a fully-fledged development model with its generally agreed upon national vision and associated array of policies, but without the requisite coordination, implementation and monitoring powers. The other countries were characterised by frequently changing national priority announcements, often around the budget speech, and a plethora of non-complementary policies in different centres of power.

In the absence of clear development models or strategies, we had to look at a range of policies from different departments, as well as medium- and long-term plans, in order to investigate whether the knowledge economy and a role for higher education in development featured. At the national level we looked at policies not only in the ministry responsible for higher education, but also in others such as economic development/planning and science and technology.

The role of knowledge and universities in national and institutional plans were operationalised into a series of indicators which are detailed in Table C1 of Appendix C. These indicators were then rated by three of the researchers for each country and university in the study. The aggregate results of these ratings are presented in the discussion of findings below.

As can be seen from Table 1, at the national level, Kenya and Mauritius exhibited the strongest awareness of the concept of the knowledge economy and a role for higher education in development, followed by Mozambique and Tanzania. However, with the exception of Mauritius, this awareness was not reflected across policies, but was predominantly found in the science and technology policy or in the long-term national vision. Most problematic, again with the exception of Mauritius, was that the concept of the knowledge economy and a role for higher education in development was mostly absent from the policies of ministries responsible for higher education. (See Box 1 for a description of the policies in Kenya and Mauritius.)

At the institutional level, we looked at the universities' strategic plans and research policies to see whether the concept of knowledge economy, and a role for the university in development, was articulated. The knowledge economy was explicitly articulated in the policies or plans of the universities of Botswana, Mauritius and Makerere (Box 1), and was absent at the University of Ghana. None of the universities had specific policies regarding the institution's role in economic development. However, this role was embedded in the strategic plan and/or research policy of the universities of Botswana, Nairobi, Mauritius and Makerere. This role was not articulated in any of the institutional documents consulted for Eduardo Mondlane, Dar es Salaam or NMMU.

TABLE 1 Role for knowledge and universities in development

Indicators	Max. score	Botswana	Ghana	Kenya	Mauritius	Moz.	South Africa	Tanzania	Uganda
NATIONAL LEVEL	6	4	3	6	6	5	4	5	4
The concept of a knowledge economy features in the national development plan	3	2	1	3	3	2	2	2	2
A role for higher education in development in national policies and plans	3	2	2	3	3	3	2	3	2
UNIVERSITY LEVEL	6	5	2	4	5	3	3	3	5
Concept of a knowledge economy features in institutional policies and plans	3	3	1	2	3	2	2	2	3
Institutional policies with regard to the university's role in economic development	3	2	1	2	2	1	1	1	2
TOTALS	12	9	5	10	11	8	7	8	9

BOX 1

The knowledge economy and role of higher education in national and institutional policies and plans

National policies and plans

In Mauritius, there was a very explicit role for higher education in development, as articulated in national policy documents such as the *Draft Education and Human Resources Strategy* and, importantly, the policies formulated in the document *Developing Mauritius into a Knowledge Hub and Centre of Learning*. As a result of the coordinated efforts of the Ministry of Education, Culture and Human Resources, and the Ministry of Finance and Economic Empowerment (MFEE), the country had made significant moves forward in translating the policy documents into implementation of the first steps to move the country towards a fully-fledged knowledge economy. In addition, the MFEE was playing an important role in the funding of a major science, technology and innovation project in the country.

In Kenya, the major education policy document, *Kenya Education Sector Support Programme*, and the Ministry of Higher Education, Science and Technology's plan for 2008-2012, were the key policy documents setting out the government's vision on the role of higher education and the commitment to the knowledge economy. The development planning document, *Kenya Vision 2030*, was helping to translate this vision into policy implementation, albeit at a somewhat slow pace.

University strategic plans and research policies

The University of Mauritius strategic plan (2006-2015) and the *Strategic Research and Innovation Framework* (2009-2015) placed the institution in a central role in contributing to the nation's economic development and consistently reflected the narrative of the knowledge economy. They emphasised research and innovation, instilling an entrepreneurial flair amongst staff and students, and linking science and technology to industry. They also aligned themselves to national policies in this regard, such as the move towards developing Mauritius into a 'knowledge hub'.

The notion of the knowledge economy and the contribution of higher education in general, and of the university in particular, to the country's national development framework were strongly foregrounded and operationalised in the University of Botswana's strategic plan. Mention was made of both the production of high-level skills, and research and innovation. The plan also took into account the changes in the economy articulated in the government's *Draft Macroeconomic Outline and Policy Framework* which highlighted the need to move away from a reliance on public sector stimulus to economic growth, and from the strong dependence on the diamond mining industry, to a stronger service sector economy, stimulated increasingly by the private sector.

Makerere University's strategic plan (2008/2009-2018/2019) tied itself closely to the institution's role in development. The formulation of the plan was guided by the question: How can Makerere University reposition itself to meet emerging development challenges in Uganda? The development of the plan took into account a range of socio-economic, political and environmental concerns. This included an overview of shifts in the Ugandan economy with specific reference to the move towards a knowledge economy and the role that Makerere can play in this regard. The plan aligned itself with a number of national policies including the *National Strategic Plan for Higher Education* and the *Uganda Poverty Eradication Action Plan*.

FINDINGS

- The most striking finding was the lack of clarity and agreement about a development model (except for Mauritius) and the role of higher education in development, at both national and institutional levels.
- None of the eight countries had a development model per se, although Mauritius was moving in that direction.
- Mauritius was also the only country that stated upfront that knowledge drives economic growth. For the other countries, knowledge was not yet considered to be key to economic development.
- There was an emerging awareness about the importance of the knowledge economy approach in all the countries and institutions. Except for Botswana and Uganda, this articulation was generally stronger at the national than at the institutional level. In addition, with the exception of Mauritius, it was seldom reflected in more than one ministry's policy, or in national vision statements.

Notions about the role of knowledge and universities

How do national and institutional stakeholders conceptualise the role of higher education and the university in development? And to what extent is there consensus or disjuncture between the national and institutional levels? Our analytical framework for addressing these questions comprised four notions of the relationship between higher education (especially universities) and national development. These four notions,[12] which are elaborated upon below, emerge in the interaction between the following two scenarios:

- Whether or not a role is foreseen for new knowledge in the national development strategy.
- Whether or not universities, as knowledge institutions, have a role in the national development strategy.

These two sets of scenarios, and the concomitant four notions of the role of universities, are depicted in Figure 1.

---

12 These four notions are based on ideas developed by Maassen and Cloete (2006) and Maassen and Olsen (2007).

FIGURE 1 **The four notions of the role of knowledge and universities in development**

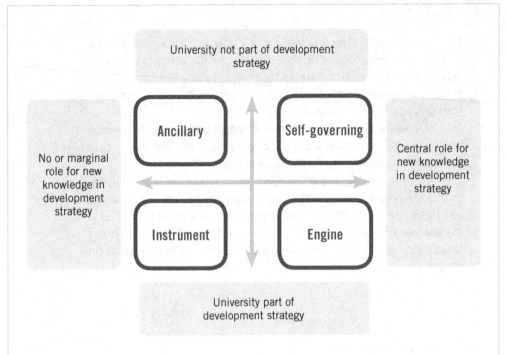

The four notions are elaborated as follows:

1. **The university as ancillary**: In this notion, there is a strong focus on political/ideological starting-points for development. Consequently, it is assumed that there is no need for a strong (scientific) knowledge basis for development strategies and policies. Neither is it necessary for the university to play a direct role in development since the emphasis is on investments in basic healthcare, agricultural production and primary education. The role of universities is to produce educated civil servants and professionals (with teaching based on transmitting established knowledge rather than on research), as well as different forms of community service.

2. **The university as self-governing institution**: Knowledge produced at the university is considered important for national development – especially for the improvement of healthcare and the strengthening of agricultural production. However, this notion assumes that the most relevant knowledge is produced when academics from the North and the South cooperate in externally-funded projects, rather than being steered by the state. This notion portrays the university as playing an important role in developing the national identity, and in producing high-level bureaucrats and scientific knowledge – but not directly related to national development; the university is committed to serving society as a whole rather than specific stakeholders. This notion assumes that the university is most effective when it is left to itself, and can

determine its own priorities according to universal criteria, independent of the particularities of a specific geographical, national, cultural or religious context. It also assumes there is no need to invest additional public funds to increase the relevance of the university.

3. **The university as instrument for development agendas**: In this notion, the university has an important role to play in national development – not through the production of new scientific knowledge, but through expertise exchange and capacity building. The focus of the university's development efforts should be on contributing to reducing poverty and disease, to improving agricultural production, and to supporting small business development – primarily through consultancy activities (especially for government agencies and development aid) and through direct involvement in local communities.

4. **The university as engine of development**: This notion assumes that knowledge plays a central role in national development – in relation to improving healthcare and agricultural production, but also in relation to innovations in the private sector, especially in areas such as information and communication technology, biotechnology and engineering. Within this notion the university is seen as (one of) the core institutions in the national development model. The underlying assumption is that the university is the only institution in society that can provide an adequate foundation for the complexities of the emerging knowledge economy when it comes to producing the relevant skills and competencies of employees in all major sectors, as well as to the production of use-oriented knowledge.

Drawing on the information above, as well as data gathered via interviews with national and university stakeholders, we now turn to an analysis of the notions of the role of knowledge and universities in each of the eight African countries.

Table 2 captures the notions of the role of knowledge and universities of both government and university stakeholders, indicating whether the notion is strong, present, or absent for each of the categories. The table also enables us to compare government and university notions in order to assess the extent to which there is consensus or disjuncture between these two sets of actors in the pact. (See Box 2 for selected quotations reflecting the different notions of the role of higher education and the university.)

At the national level there are three main observations. Firstly, the instrumental notion was the strongest, followed by engine of development and self-governing. Secondly, the engine of development notion was to be found mainly in science and technology policies and in national vision statements, but seldom in ministries of education – with the exceptions of Botswana and Mauritius. The references to knowledge economy, and its importance in vision statements, seem to draw considerably from 'policy-borrowing', particularly from World Bank and OECD sources and websites. Thirdly, in the case of the instrumental notion, most national government officials felt that universities were not doing enough, but there were no policies that spell out, or incentivise, this instrumental role.

TABLE 2 National and institutional notions of the role of the university in development

Notions	Ancillary		Self-governing		Instrument		Engine	
Country	Government	University	Government	University	Government	University	Government	University
Botswana	•	•	□	□	■	□	□	□
Ghana	■	□	□	■	•	•	□	•
Kenya	•	•	□	■	□	■	■	□
Mauritius	•	•	□	□	■	□	■	■
Mozambique	•	•	□	■	■	□	□	•
South Africa	•	□	■	□	■	□	□	□
Tanzania	■	□	•	□	■	■	□	•
Uganda	•	•	□	■	■	■	•	□

Key:

■ Strong   □ Present   • Absent

Regarding the institutional notions the following observations could be made. Firstly, self-governance and the instrumental roles were the strongest positions, which reflect the traditional debates about autonomy and community engagement, respectively. This emphasis on the self-governing notion could be because the university leadership was more concerned with traditional university issues, while governments tended to be more focused on global trends. Secondly, only within the universities of Ghana and Dar es Salaam was there still a fairly traditional notion of the university producing personpower for the nation, and of the university 'knowing best what is required'. Interestingly, the leadership of neither of these two institutions expressed a knowledge economy discourse. Thirdly, Mauritius was the only institution with the engine of development as the dominant discourse, and it corresponded with the view of government. At Makerere there was considerable agreement between government and the university, except that there was an increasing awarenss at the university about the knowledge economy and the engine of development notion. Finally, at NMMU, which is an institution where a former 'traditional' university was merged with a technikon (polytechnic), all four notions were present and in contestation.

BOX 2

Selected narratives on the role of the university in development

I think really right from the beginning, this being the first national university, the focus had been to play a leading role in providing the necessary human capital for driving this nation. And you will see then from the Sixties, the government gave such a mandate to this university to train the critical manpower – not only to take over the positions that the foreigners were leaving, going back, but also to drive development. (University leader)

The discussion about the identity of the institution and the philosophy of education reveals a number of tensions: one body of opinion argues that the university should essentially focus on more practical, vocational training that will hopefully generate students that can find quicker employment and make a difference out there. There's another part coming from the old part of the university arguing that we should focus on more medium- and long-term development goals ... Those fault lines of debate are still very much present in the institution now. (University leader)

I think the fact that the new government separated higher education from science for me was the first sign that they really don't understand higher education. They don't understand the system. They know it's powerful, they know it's important, they know that they have to invest, but honestly I don't think they understand what higher education is all about. (Senior academic)

We firmly believe in Mauritius that knowledge drives economic growth and development. Higher education is the main source of that knowledge and of human capital. It is the knowledge promoter required for the social and economic development of any country. (National stakeholder)

FINDINGS

- In terms of notions of the role of the university in development, at both national and institutional levels, the most obvious unresolved tension was between the self-governance and instrumental roles. This reflects the well-known tension between institutional autonomy, on the one hand, and engagement or responsiveness, on the other.
- At the national level in most of the countries, the dominant expectation from higher education was an instrumental role, with a constant refrain that the university was not doing enough to contribute to development – but often referring to social problems, and not economic growth.
- The engine of development notion was stronger amongst government stakeholders than within the universities, but it could be that government saw knowledge as a narrow instrumental, rather than an engine of development notion. It is nevertheless surprising that amongst university leadership the support for a knowledge economy approach was so weak.

3

The academic core
of eight African universities

The university's unique contribution to development is via knowledge – transmitting knowledge to individuals who will go out into the labour market and contribute to society in a variety of ways (teaching), and producing and disseminating knowledge that can lead to innovation or be applied to the problems of society and economy (research, engagement). Part of our analytical framework for understanding what impacts on a university's ability to make a sustainable contribution to development therefore focuses on the nature and strength of its knowledge activities.

According to Burton Clark (1998), when an enterprising university evolves a stronger steering core and develops an outreach structure, its heartland is still in the traditional academic departments, formed around disciplines and some interdisciplinary fields. The heartland is where traditional academic values and activities such as teaching, research and training of the next generation of academics occur. Instead of 'heartland', we use the concept 'academic core'. According to our analytical assumption, it is this core that needs to be strong and relevant if flagship universities – such as those included in this study – as key knowledge institutions, are to contribute to development.

While most universities also engage in knowledge activities in the area of community service or outreach, our contention was that the backbone or the foundation of the university's business is its academic core – that is, the basic handling of knowledge through teaching via academic degree programmes, research output, and the production of doctorates (those who, in the future, will be responsible for carrying out the core knowledge activities).

Our interest in the academic core of the eight universities in this study had the following two dimensions:

1. What is the strength of the academic cores of these universities?
2. Has there been a strengthening or weakening of these academic cores in recent years?

As mentioned, the eight African universities included in the study were Botswana, Dar es Salaam, Eduardo Mondlane, Ghana, Makerere, Mauritius, Nairobi and Nelson Mandela Metropolitan University. With the exception of NMMU, all of these institutions were considered flagship universities and were rated number one in their respective countries. These institutions were the leading knowledge-producing institutions expected to make a contribution to research and development. This is well expressed in the University of Botswana research strategy (2008: 3) as follows:

The university has the largest concentration of research-qualified staff and research facilities in the country and has an obligation to develop the full potential of these resources. By doing so, it can play a central part in the multiple strategies for promoting research, development and innovation that are now on the national agenda.

A review of the vision and mission statements of these eight universities revealed a number of common aims relating to both the nature and strength of their academic cores, as well as their contribution to development. These aims might be summarised as follows:

- To have high academic ratings, making them leading or premier universities – not only in their respective countries but also in Africa;
- To be centres of academic excellence which are engaged in high-quality research and scholarship; and
- To contribute to sustainable national and regional social and economic development.

The question is: did the evidence support these ambitious aims for academic excellence? In other words, was there evidence that these universities have strong academic cores or, at the very least, were moving in that direction?

In this section, we present and discuss the findings of the analysis of data pertaining to the academic cores of the eight universities. NMMU was selected for the South African case study based on its comparability in terms of size and profile to the other seven institutions. Given that NMMU did not have flagship status as such, and in order to provide an 'African benchmark', we included the University of Cape Town as a ninth institution in the analysis below: Cape Town was the number one ranked university in South Africa and in Africa at the time of the study. We begin with a brief overview of the methodology employed in collecting and analysing the data.

3.1 Methodology

CHET started compiling data on a group of African universities in 2007 as part of a project called *Cross-National Higher Education Performance (Efficiency) Indicators*.[13] The data collected subsequent to this was discussed at a workshop in March 2009, where it emerged that although a basic data set had been compiled from institutional representatives and planners, most of the universities had experienced difficulties in completing the 2007 data templates. For a more detailed discussion on data problems encountered at the institutions, see Appendix D. Suffice to say that the first finding about the academic core was that there was a need to improve and strengthen the definition of key performance indicators, as well as the systematic, institution-wide capturing and processing (institutionalisation) of key performance indicator data.

---

13   Website: http://www.chet.org.za/programmes/indicators/.

In order to rate the strength of the academic core of the universities in the study, the following eight indicators were identified, all of which refer to characteristics or activities that reflect the production of high-quality scholarship which, in turn, forms the basis of each university's potential contribution to development. The eight indicators, and the rationale for their inclusion, are outlined below. They were divided into five input and three output indicators. Some of these indicators were based on traditional notions of the role of flagship universities (e.g. the production of new knowledge and the next generation of academics) while others (e.g. science, engineering and technology enrolments and student–staff ratios) were pertinent to the African context.

Input indicators:
1. **Increased enrolments in science, engineering and technology (SET):** In African governments and foreign development agencies alike, there was a strong emphasis on SET as important drivers of development (Juma & Yee-Cheong 2005). Included in SET are the agricultural sciences, architecture and urban and regional planning, computer and information science, health sciences and veterinary sciences, life sciences and physical sciences.
2. **Increased postgraduate enrolments:** The knowledge economy and universities are demanding increasing numbers of people with postgraduate qualifications.
3. **A favourable academic staff to student ratio:** The academic workload should allow for the possibility of research and PhD supervision.
4. **A high proportion of academic staff with doctoral degrees:** Research (CHET 2010) has shown that there is a high correlation between staff with doctorates, on the one hand, and research output and the training of PhD students, on the other.
5. **Adequate research funding per academic:** Research requires government and institutional funding and 'third-stream' funding from external sources such as industry and foreign donors.

Output indicators:
6. **High graduation rates in SET fields:** Not only is it important to increase SET enrolments, it is crucial that universities achieve high graduation rates in order to respond to the skills shortages in the African labour market in these fields.
7. **Increased knowledge production in the form of doctoral graduates:** There is a need for an increase in doctoral graduates for two reasons. Firstly, doctoral graduates form the backbone of academia and are therefore critical for the future reproduction of the academic core. Secondly, there is growing demand for people with doctoral degrees outside of academia (e.g. in research organisations and other organisations such as financial institutions).
8. **Knowledge production in the form of research publications in recognised ISI journals:** Academics need to be producing peer-reviewed research publications in order for the university to participate in the global knowledge community and to contribute to new knowledge and innovation.

We now present the summary data and ratings for the institutions included in the sample, as well as a discussion of the findings. (See Table E1 in Appendix E which shows how each of the indicators was calculated, and how the ratings were constructed.)

3.2   The academic core data

Table 3 presents the basic academic core data for the universities in the sample, indicating the changes between 2001 and 2007. Table 4 presents an overview of the ratings (or scores) per university for each of the academic core indicators. The values of the input and output indicators in Table 4 are rated as either 'strong', 'medium' or 'weak'. The first three input and the three output data elements are averages for the seven-year period 2001–2007. The remaining two input indicators are based on data which were available only for 2007. Table 5 provides the average annual growth rates over the period 2001–2007.

This data set (Tables 3, 4 and 5) provides comparative data for the universities in our sample. In addition, it could be used by institutions in the eight countries as a benchmark for their own performance.

The data indicate that, apart from NMMU and Ghana, each of the universities had at least one 'strong' rating. Cape Town was rated 'strong' for all eight indicators, Mauritius for four of the eight, Dar es Salaam and Nairobi for three of the eight, and Botswana, Eduardo and Makerere for two of the eight indicators.

A large number of 'weak' ratings appear in the scores of different universities. Eduardo was rated as 'weak' on six of the eight indicators; Botswana and Ghana on five of the eight indicators. Makerere and Nairobi were rated as 'weak' on four of the eight indicators, and Mauritius on three of the eight indicators. NMMU had two 'weak' ratings and Cape Town none.

On the input side, Cape Town's overall rating was 'strong', and those of Dar es Salaam, Mauritius and Nairobi were about mid-way between 'strong' and 'medium'. Two universities, Makerere and NMMU, had overall input ratings which were close to the average 'medium' rating. Three universities – Botswana, Eduardo and Ghana – had overall input ratings mid-way between 'weak' and 'medium'. On the output side, Cape Town's average rating was 'strong', and no other university had output ratings of above 'medium', except NMMU had a 'medium' rating. The remaining seven universities had overall output ratings below the 'medium' rating.

From these scores the institutions can be broadly categorised into the following groups:

- Group 1 contains Cape Town which is the only university which was 'strong' on all input and output ratings.
- Group 2 contains Mauritius, Makerere and NMMU which had 'medium' or 'strong' ratings on both the input and the output sides.
- Group 3 contains Dar es Salaam, Nairobi and Botswana which had overall 'medium' and 'strong' ratings on the input side, but which were 'weak' on the output side.
- Group 4 contains Ghana and Eduardo Mondlane which had 'weak' ratings on both the input and the output side.

TABLE 3 Academic core indicators: Scores and changes (2001–2007)

University	% SET enrolments 2001	% SET enrolments 2007	Masters enrolments 2001	Masters enrolments 2007	Doctoral enrolments 2001	Doctoral enrolments 2007	Student-staff ratios 2001	Student-staff ratios 2007	Student-staff ratios 2007 SET	Student-staff ratios 2007 BUS[1]	Doctoral graduates 2001	Doctoral graduates 2007	Research publications 2001	Research publications 2007	Research publications per academic 2001	Research publications per academic 2007
Cape Town	40%	42%	2 788	2 906	706	1 002	12	15	22	42	86	102	700	1 017	0.92	1.14
Botswana	22%	22%	493	951	8	41	14	27	10	59	3	4	69	106	0.10	0.14
Dar es Salaam	52%	36%	609	2 165	54	190	11	14	14	22	10	20	49	70	0.12	0.07
Eduardo Mondlane[2]	61%	48%	0	420	0	3	10	13	12	51	0	0	0	11	0.03	0.03
Ghana	22%	18%	1 344	1 580	69	102	12	31	9	68	2	20	77	61	0.12	0.08
Makerere	16%	32%	1 167	2 767	28	32	15	18	11	96	11	23	72	139	0.07	0.20
Mauritius	51%	43%	350	859	114	193	24	16	12	34	7	10	23	36	0.12	0.13
Nairobi	33%	31%	3 937	6 145	190	62	12	18	8	42	26	32	143	136	0.12	0.11
NMMU	18%	31%	1 100	1 332	175	327	31	28	26	54	27	35	154	180	0.30	0.34

Notes:

1. BUS = Business
2. 2001 figures for Eduardo Mondlane for masters and doctoral enrolments, and doctoral graduates and research publications, were not provided by the institution.

TABLE 4 Academic core indicators: Ratings per university

	INPUT INDICATORS					OUTPUT INDICATORS		
PERIOD >>	Average for 2001–2007			2007 only			Average for 2001–2007	
INDICATOR >>	% SET enrolments	% Masters and doctoral enrolments	Student-staff ratios	% Academics with doctoral degrees	Research income/permanent academic (ppp$)*	SET graduation rate	Doctoral graduates as % of permanent academics	Ratio of research publications/permanent academic
RATING >>	Strong: >39% Medium: 30–39% Weak: <30%	Strong: >9% Medium: 5–9% Weak: <5%	Strong: <20 Medium: 20–30 Weak: >30	Strong: >49% Medium: 30–49% Weak: <30%	Strong: >20 000 Medium: 10 000–20 000 Weak: <10 000	Strong: >20% Medium: 17–20% Weak: <17%	Strong: >10% Medium: 5–10% Weak: <5%	Strong: >0.5 Medium: 0.25–0.5 Weak: <0.25
Cape Town	41%	19%	13	58%	47 700	21%	15.00%	0.95
Botswana	22%	5%	15	31%	2 000	20%	0.66%	0.11
Dar es Salaam	43%	9%	14	50%	6 400	19%	2.18%	0.08
Eduardo Mondlane	54%	2%	12	24%	0	6%	0.00%	0.03
Ghana	19%	7%	22	47%	3 400	18%	0.17%	0.09
Makerere	24%	5%	16	31%	4 900	22%	1.63%	0.09
Mauritius	48%	13%	17	45%	3 000	26%	2.80%	0.13
Nairobi	31%	16%	14	71%	5 300	17%	1.87%	0.09
NMMU	25%	6%	30	34%	12 300	18%	5.50%	0.31

Key:

▨ Strong ▨ Medium ☐ Weak

* The 'research income per permanent academic' figures are calculated as PPP$ (purchasing power parity dollar) amounts. Some of these figures are based on estimates as not all of the universities were able to provide reliable research income data. The source of information upon which each figure is based is indicated below the academic core rating table for each university in Part 3.

TABLE 5 Academic core indicators: Average annual growth rates (2001–2007)

University	SET enrolments	Masters enrolments	Doctoral enrolments	Doctoral graduates	Research publications
Cape Town	3.1%	0.7%	6.0%	2.9%	6.4%
Botswana	5.3%	11.6%	31.3%	4.9%	7.4%
Dar es Salaam	8.3%	23.5%	23.3%	12.2%	6.1%
Eduardo Mondlane	6.6%	n/a	n/a	n/a	n/a
Ghana	12.9%	2.7%	6.7%	46.8%	-3.8%
Makerere	16.3%	15.5%	2.3%	13.1%	11.6%
Mauritius	2.2%	16.1%	9.2%	6.1%	7.8%
Nairobi	7.6%	7.7%	-17.0%	3.5%	-0.8%
NMMU	3.7%	3.2%	11.0%	4.4%	2.6%

Note: Annual growth rates for Eduardo Mondlane are not available in the table above for masters and doctoral enrolments, and doctoral graduates and research publications, because the institution could not provide us with this information for 2001.

3.3 The strength of and changes in the academic cores

The data indicate that with the exception of Cape Town, the other universities did not have academic cores that live up to the high expectations contained in their mission statements. However, the data show considerable variance amongst the institutions in terms of input indicators, and some convergence regarding output indicators, with the exception of Cape Town.

Two input indicators with considerable variation were student–staff ratios and permanent academics with doctorates. With regard to the student–staff ratio, two institutions managed to decrease the instruction loads of their academic staff (Mauritius: ratio of 24:1 in 2001 to 16:1 in 2007; NMMU: 31:1 down to 28:1) (Table 3). The student-to-academic staff ratio at Ghana increased substantially from 12:1 in 2001 to 31:1 in 2007, as did that of Botswana from 14:1 in 2001 to 27:1 in 2007 (Table 3). The ratios at other institutions increased, but not dramatically: Nairobi (12–18), Makerere (15–18), Eduardo (10–13), Dar es Salaam (11–14) and Cape Town (12–15) (Table 3).

These ratios do not support the stereotype of 'mass overcrowding' in African higher education; certainly not at the flagship universities. While one institution (Ghana) had a ratio of over 30:1, six institutions were under 20:1 (Table 3). But, these gross figures obscure substantial variations within the fields of study offered by institutions (Table 3). For example, at Nairobi, the student–staff ratio in 2007 in SET was 8:1 while it was 42:1 in business. More unfavourable examples were Ghana where the 2007 SET ratio was 9:1 and the business ratio was 68:1, and Makerere where the 2007 SET ratio was 11:1 and the business ratio 96:1. More 'normal' variations were at Cape Town which, in 2007, had a 22:1 ratio for SET and 42:1 for business, and Dar es Salaam which had 14:1 for SET and 22:1 for business.

A study by CHET (2010) on higher education differentiation showed that in South Africa there is a highly significant correlation of 0.82 between the proportion of the academic staff of a university that has a doctorate as their highest qualification and the research publications produced at that university. This implies that it is only in exceptional cases that academics without a doctorate publish in internationally-recognised research-reviewed journals or books.

The data in Table 4 show that in 2007 three universities had proportions of permanent academics with doctorates of 50% or higher. They were Nairobi (71%), Cape Town (58%) and Dar es Salaam (50%). This is very strong capacity – in South Africa, only three of 23 universities in 2007 had a proportion of 50% or higher of permanent academic staff with doctorates. Ghana, Makerere, Mauritius and NMMU had, in 2007, proportions of permanent academic staff with doctorates in the band 30% to 49%. Unfortunately, we did not have trend data for this indicator so we cannot comment on whether the percentages of staff with doctorates were increasing or decreasing.

The three output indicators in this study are SET graduation rates, doctoral graduates and publications in ISI-recognised journals. Starting with SET graduation rates, an average annual ratio of 25% SET graduates to SET enrolments is roughly equivalent to a cohort graduation rate of 75%, a ratio of 20% is equivalent to a cohort graduation rate of 60%, and a ratio of 15% is equivalent to a cohort graduation rate of 45%. The SET graduation rates (Table 4) show that Botswana, Makerere, Mauritius and Cape Town all had rates of at least 60% of the cohort of students graduating, while Dar es Salaam's was just under 60%. The rest were under 50%. Eduardo Mondlane, which had the highest proportion of enrolments in SET (54% of its enrolments during 2001–2007), had the poorest graduation rate.

Doctoral output was very low. Five of the universities (Botswana, Dar es Salaam, Ghana, Mauritius and Eduardo) produced 20 or fewer doctorates in 2007, while three (Makerere, Nairobi and NMMU) produced between 20 and 40, and Cape Town over 100 (Table 3). Most worrisome is that amongst all the institutions, the growth in doctoral graduations was below 10%, with the exceptions of Ghana, Dar es Salaam and Makerere, which grew from a very low base (Table 5). At the University of Nairobi, doctoral enrolments declined by 17%.

The slow growth in doctoral enrolments is in sharp contrast to the 'explosion' of masters enrolments (Table 5). At Dar es Salaam, enrolment of masters increased by 23.5% (from 609 in 2001 to 2 165 in 2007). Three other universities (Mauritius, Makerere and Botswana) had average annual increases of higher than 10% between 2001 and 2007. At the other universities growth was below 10%, with Cape Town growing less than 1% (Table 5).

As was indicated above, the fast growth in masters enrolment was not matched by a commensurate expansion in doctoral studies. For example, at Nairobi, masters enrolments between 2001 and 2007 grew at an average annual rate of 7.7% while doctoral enrolments declined. At Makerere, masters enrolments grew at an annual rate of 15.5%, while doctoral enrolments grew at only 2.3% (Table 5). The continuation rates from masters to doctoral studies seem absurdly low in certain cases. An ideal ratio of masters to doctoral enrolments should be at least 5:1, which is an indication that masters graduates flow into doctoral research programmes. In 2007, Cape Town, Mauritius and NMMU all had ratios of masters to doctoral students below 4:1. Botswana, Dar es Salaam and Ghana all had ratios between 10:1 to 23:1, while the other three – Eduardo Mondlane, Makerere and Nairobi – had ratios above 50:1.[14]

Regarding research publications, it was assumed that a flagship knowledge producer must produce research-based academic articles that can be published in internationally peer-reviewed journals and/or books. The target for permanent academics was set at one research article to be published every two years, which translates into an annual ratio of 0.50 research publications per academic. In our sample, which deals with average ratios for the period 2001–2007, only Cape Town (with an average of 0.95) met this requirement (Table 4). With the exceptions of NMMU (0.31) and Mauritius (0.13), the ratios of the other universities imply that on average each of their permanent academics was likely to publish only one research article every 10 or more years.

From the above it is evident that particularly the output variables of the universities were not strong enough to make a sustainable knowledge production contribution to development. Nevertheless, there were some positive trends in this worrisome picture. The majority of universities had strong input performance in academics with doctorates, student–staff ratios, and an increase in enrolments at the masters level. On the output side, the graduation rate of SET was quite strong for most of the institutions. There was also an increase in research output, albeit from a very low base. In 2007, Makerere produced the third highest total of research publications (139) in the sample, after Cape Town with 1 017 and NMMU with 180. Makerere showed an 11.6% growth in publication output over the seven-year period, Mauritius 7.8%, Botswana 7.4% and Dar 6.1% (Table 5). At Ghana and Nairobi, the output of ISI-accredited publications declined.

However, it should also be noted that even though the research productivity in terms of academic articles produced was increasing at the universities included, since the productivity in the rest of the world was increasing much faster, the relative position of Africa as knowledge producer was decreasing gradually. Sub-Saharan Africa contributes around 0.7% to world scientific output, and this figure has decreased over the last 15 to 20 years (French Academy of Sciences 2006).

3.4   Disjunctures between capacity and productivity

There is a long-held commonsense view that the lack of research output in African universities is simply a lack of capacity and resources. However, a closer inspection of the input-output indicators raises some interesting questions about this assumption. In order to explore this further, we selected Cape Town from group 1, Dar es Salaam from group 3 and Ghana from group 4 as representatives of these groups and plotted a comparative graph based on standardised scores (Figure 2).

---

14   These masters-to-doctoral enrolment and graduation ratios are contained in the individual case study reports for the respective universities.

The data showed that there were surprising similarities between Dar es Salaam and Cape Town in terms of input indicators such as SET enrolments (Cape Town 41%, Dar es Salaam 40%), student–staff ratio (Cape Town 13:1, Dar es Salaam 14:1) and academics with PhDs (Cape Town 58%, Dar es Salaam 50%). Ghana, on the other hand, was only similar to the other two in terms of staff qualifications. On the input side, the big difference between Cape Town, on the one hand, and Dar es Salaam and Ghana on the other, was in percentage of postgraduate students (Cape Town 19% versus Dar es Salaam 9% and Ghana 7%) and research income per permanent staff member (Cape Town PPP$ 47 700 versus Dar es Salaam PPP$ 6 400 and Ghana PPP$ 3 400).

FIGURE 2 **Academic core indicators (standardised data): Three selected universities**

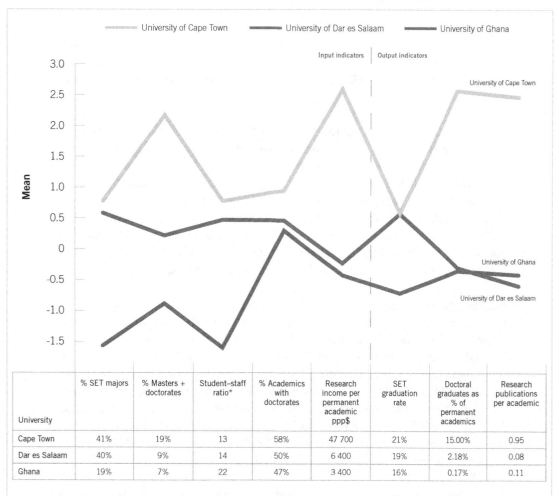

University	% SET majors	% Masters + doctorates	Student–staff ratio*	% Academics with doctorates	Research income per permanent academic ppp$	SET graduation rate	Doctoral graduates as % of permanent academics	Research publications per academic
Cape Town	41%	19%	13	58%	47 700	21%	15.00%	0.95
Dar es Salaam	40%	9%	14	50%	6 400	19%	2.18%	0.08
Ghana	19%	7%	22	47%	3 400	16%	0.17%	0.11

* In the data table the student–staff ratio is given, whilst the inverse of the student–staff ratio has been used in the graph representing the results of the k-means clustering. This was done because a high student–staff value is unfavourable and should thus reflect a low value in the k-means clustering. The University of Ghana has a high value for student–staff value in the table but the inverse shows a low value in the graph of the means for the clustering.

With regard to output indicators, Cape Town and Dar es Salaam had similar SET graduation rates (21% and 19%, respectively). The dramatic difference was in doctoral graduates (average for 2001–2007): Cape Town 15% of academic staff, and Dar es Salaam and Ghana less than 3% per academic staff member (Figure 2), and ISI publications (2007): Cape Town 1 017, Ghana 61 and Dar es Salaam 70 (Table 3).

This data poses some intriguing issues for higher education in Africa. Cape Town and Dar es Salaam had remarkably similar profiles in terms of SET (input and output), student–staff ratios and staff with doctorates, but were incomparable regarding the production of doctorates and publications. What distinguished Cape Town from the other institutions was much higher proportions of postgraduates, research income and knowledge production outputs.

In terms of input capacity, Cape Town and Dar es Salaam were surprisingly similar, with the exception of research income (resources). Does that mean that research income was the only factor that prevented Dar es Salaam from achieving the same level of outputs as Cape Town?

During interviews with senior academics, three factors emerged that raised questions and warranted further research. The first was the problem of research funding. Not only was there very limited research funding, but the cumbersome application procedures and the restrictions on what the research funds could be used for made consultancy money much more attractive; in particular, consultancy money directly supplemented academics' income, and the researchers also had much more discretion about how it was used. The negative side of consultancy funds was that there was no pressure or expectation to publish, nor to train postgraduate students. It thus affected negatively both aspects of knowledge production, that is, postgraduate training and publishing.

Incentives to publish, as is the case in many countries, was a problem. After obtaining the professorship, publishing in international journals was not directly rewarded, but was rather a matter of prestige or 'institutional culture'. In order to incentivise this activity, universities in Africa might have to start exploring incentive systems. In South Africa, the national government subsidised each institution to the tune of about USD 45 000 per PhD graduate and USD 15 000 per accredited publication. But this is not a simple correlation. Two of the universities with the highest publication rates per permanent academic (Cape Town and Rhodes) did not pass a portion of the subsidy directly to the academic or the department, but add it to their general operational budgets for the direct and indirect support of teaching.

Another dimension that certainly warrants further exploration is the relationship between research and consultancy. A PhD study by Langa (2010) suggests that having a strong academic network link, with publications, is an entry for getting consultancies. So it is not that academics choose research or consultancy; some do a balancing act between research and consultancy, while others seem to 'drift off' into consultancy and foreign aid networks.

A second problem that is affecting the production of doctorates, and associated research training and publication, is the huge increase in taught masters courses which do not lead to doctoral study. For example, the University of Cape Town had 2 906 masters enrolments and 1 002 doctoral enrolments in 2007. In contrast, in 2007 Dar es Salaam had 2 165 masters students and only 190 doctoral enrolments (Table 3). This means that there was a serious 'pipeline' problem at universities like Dar es Salaam. This could be because the masters degree does not inspire sufficient confidence in students to enrol for the PhD, or because there were no incentives to do so, or because individuals were pursuing their PhD degrees abroad. Whatever the reason, the effect was a serious curtailing of PhD numbers and hence of an essential ingredient in the knowledge production process.

According to the discussions with interview respondents, the third factor that distracts academics from knowledge production is supplementary teaching. On the one hand, the new method of raising third-stream income – namely, the innovation of private and public students in the same institution, with additional remuneration for teaching the private students – had the result that within the university, academics were teaching more to supplement their incomes. On the other hand, the proliferation of private higher education institutions, some literally within walking distance of public institutions, meant that large numbers of senior academics were 'triple teaching'.

PhD supervision, in a context where the candidate in all likelihood does not have funds for full-time study and where there are no extrinsic (only intrinsic) institutional rewards, is a poor competitor for the time of the triple-teaching academic. The same applies to rigorous research required for international peer-reviewed publication: it is much easier and far more rewarding to triple teach and do consultancies.

The implication of the above is that the lack of knowledge production at Africa's flagship universities is not a simple lack of capacity and resources, but a complex set of capacities and contradictory rewards within a resource-scarce situation. This results in a fundamental lack of a strong output-oriented research culture at these universities.

FINDINGS

- Except for the University of Cape Town, the knowledge production output variables of the academic cores were not strong enough to enable universities to make a sustainable contribution to development.
- None of the universities in the sample seemed to be moving significantly from their traditional undergraduate teaching role to a strong academic core that could contribute to new knowledge production and, by implication, to development.

FINDINGS ctd...

- Amongst the universities there was considerable diversity regarding input variables. The weakest indicators were the low proportion of postgraduate enrolments and the inadequate research funds for permanent staff, with the strongest input indicators in manageable student–staff ratios and well-qualified staff.
- On the output side, SET graduation rates were generally positive. But there was a convergence around low knowledge production, particularly doctoral graduation rates and ISI-cited publications.
- The most serious challenges to strengthening the academic core seemed to be the lack of research funds and low knowledge production (PhD graduates and peer-reviewed publications).
- The low knowledge production could not be blamed solely on low capacity and resources; the problematic incentive structures at these universities require further study.
- There is a clearly identified need to improve and strengthen the definition of key performance indicators, as well as the systematic, institution-wide capturing and processing (institutionalisation) of key performance indicator data.

We continue to explore some of these and other issues relating to the strength or otherwise of the academic core in the next section, where we undertake an analysis of a selection of development-related projects and their relationship to the academic core of the eight universities in the broader study.

4
Coordination and connectedness

As highlighted earlier, our analytical framework proposed that the following three interrelated factors need to be in place in order for universities to make a sustainable contribution to development: agreement amongst the major actors (pact) about the role of universities in development; academic core capacity in universities; and coordination of and connectedness between the policies and activities of government, universities and external groupings.

In this section we focus on the latter aspects of coordination and connectedness. In this study 'coordination' was used to refer to more structured forms of interaction, mainly between government and institutions; in other words, the knowledge policies and implementation activities of different government departments, particularly departments of education, science and technology, and research councils.

Knowledge policies have become increasingly important in the context of the knowledge economy. Broadly speaking, knowledge policies refer to political mechanisms (such as policies and incentives) that are aimed at improving the (knowledge) capacity of a country to participate in the global knowledge economy. Such policies thus relate to the higher education and science and technology sectors, and to high-level skills training, research and innovation. The coordination of knowledge policies can take place at the level of both policy formulation and policy implementation. Braun (2008) distinguishes between 'negative' and 'positive' coordination. He defines negative coordination as follows (Braun 2008: 230):

> [Where] actors – for example, two ministries – are not completely independent in their decision-making but obliged to take into account a negative backlash against their own actions by the other actor. ... Negative coordination is a non-cooperative game that leads ... to the mutual adjustment of actors, but not to concerted action nor to cohesiveness of policies.

Positive coordination goes beyond mutual adjustment: 'Instead, actors start to cooperate with each other in order to deliver certain services ... It typically develops at the ministerial or agency level' (ibid.). Positive coordination is a necessary but not sufficient condition for effective policy coordination. What is required is 'policy integration' (the coordination of goals) and 'strategic coordination' ('the development of encompassing common visions and strategies for the future') (ibid.: 230–231). These last two types of coordination point to the need for consensus or a pact. As Braun (ibid.: 230) observes: 'Policy coordination as such does not absolutely need a whole-government perspective, but it implies at a minimum a perspective that is agreed upon by a number of political actors.'

Of specific interest to this study was the coordination of knowledge policies across ministries involved with higher education, science, technology and innovation, as well as those responsible for economic development or planning.

Implementation can be regarded as a component of the coordination of government policies and is a complex combination of agreement (relevant parties support the policy) and capacity to design and apply the implementation mechanisms or instruments. At the national level we looked at the role of the ministry responsible for higher education, steering and funding. At the university level, indicators were used that dealt with aspects such as units or structures to implement strategic plans, incentives and rewards, special teaching and research programmes that link to economic development and funding support for research.

We used the concept of 'connectedness' to depict looser forms of interaction such as the linkages and networking between the university and external groupings including business, foreign donors and community groups or agencies. We also explored the extent to which 44 development projects or centres identified by institutional leadership were connected to external groupings in ways that either strengthened or weakened the academic core of the universities.

In this section, we address the following three questions:

1. Do governments coordinate policies and programmes that are aimed at enabling the universities to contribute to development?
2. Do the universities connect to external groupings in ways that promote development?
3. Do development activities in the universities strengthen or weaken their academic core?

4.1   Coordination and implementation of knowledge policies

National coordination

In this section, we present and discuss findings regarding the extent to which there was coordination of knowledge policies and activities at the national level. Table 6 summarises the ratings of the coordination indicators for the eight African countries and universities in the study (see Table C2 in Appendix C for an elaboration of these indicators). As can be seen from Table 6, Mauritius rated the highest at both national and institutional levels.

The two countries that scored highest on knowledge policies – Mauritius and Kenya (Table 1, section 2.1) – also had the highest rating for coordinating policies and building agreement at the national level (Table 6 and Box 3). To this list is added South Africa. The most common structure for promoting coordination and consensus-building was forums. However, feedback from interviewees suggested that these were seldom more than talk shops; follow-up to agreements were weak and there were few attempts at monitoring progress and the implementation of decisions. Even in countries such as South Africa, where there are stronger forms of coordination such as ministerial clusters, the same lack of follow-through occurred. In other cases, the efficacy of the structure was undermined by different departments sending officials of different ranks to meetings, leading to a gradual loss of confidence in the structure. The exception was Mauritius, where considerable effort was being made with multiple structures and networks to broaden agreement and buy-in.

TABLE 6 Coordination of knowledge policies

Indicators	Max. score	Botswana	Ghana	Kenya	Mauritius	Moz.	South Africa	Tanzania	Uganda
NATIONAL LEVEL	**9**	**3**	**3**	**6**	**7**	**4**	**6**	**4**	**3**
Economic development and higher education planning are linked	**3**	1	1	2	3	1	2	1	1
Coordination and consensus building of government agencies involved in higher education	**3**	1	1	2	2	1	2	1	1
Link between universities and national authorities	**3**	1	1	2	2	2	2	2	1

There was also evidence of attempts at coordination through the creation of 'super-ministries'. For instance in Mauritius, in order to implement plans to turn the country into a knowledge hub, a Ministry of Education and Scientific Research was created. This was then reorganised into the Ministry of Education, Culture and Human Resources and, in May 2010, reorganised once again into the Ministry of Tertiary Education, Science, Research and Technology. Kenya also established a Ministry of Higher Education, Science and Technology in 2008 (although, according to one interviewee, this had more to do with coalition politics than it did with attempts at policy coordination). Mozambique, in line with a very advanced science, technology and innovation policy, established a Ministry of Higher Education, Science and Technology in 2000 but, in 2009, dissolved it into separate ministries of Education, and Science and Technology. South Africa, having a very sophisticated policy in the Department of Science and Technology, but not in Education, recently established a Ministry of Higher Education and Training, keeping a clear separation between science and higher education. A perpetual problem in the countries investigated, and in many international systems, was the absence of cooperation (Braun's 'negative coordination') between departments of education and science and technology – but merging them did not seem to guarantee positive policy coordination either.

In terms of the interaction between universities and government, in all three of the 'successful' systems (Pillay 2010b), networks played an important 'connecting' role. In North Carolina the networks seemed to be stronger than the structures, while in South Korea there were both formal structures coordinated under the prime minister's office, and networks of academics and business leaders who had studied at particular universities such as the University of Seoul and abroad – mainly in the US. These networks were both political and productive, meaning they also fostered collaboration on projects and new initiatives.

Five of the eight African countries in the study (Mauritius, Mozambique, South Africa, Tanzania and Kenya) had some form of structure or platform for linking universities to government, although these did not necessarily result in effective coordination (Box 3). What we observed in our sample of African countries was a strong connection between university and government leadership, although it seemed more orientated towards the political than to the productive. It could be argued that the two were actually too close, because we encountered the constant refrain of policy instability, meaning that when there was a political leadership change in government, it affected both government departments and the university. Policy reversals, and associated staff changes described above in Mozambique, was an exacerbated example.

In response to weak ministries, and in following international best practices, all the countries in the sample had established higher or tertiary education councils, which were, with few exceptions, better resourced than the national ministries – and were more distant from direct ministerial influence. These structures were better placed and resourced than traditional ministries to play a coordinating role. However, these relatively new organisations were all going through some form of 'role redefinition'; most were started as quality/certification bodies, but as was the case, for example, in Botswana, Mauritius and Tanzania, they were increasingly assuming a diversity of roles – from system planning to leadership capacity building and in, some cases, even making funding allocations.

BOX 3

COORDINATION OF KNOWLEDGE POLICIES AND ACTIVITIES

Linking economic and higher education planning

In none of the eight African countries was there an explicit link between economic and higher education planning. In Mauritius, the history of economic development over the past two decades suggests the existence of informal structures that ensure a high degree of linkage between economic and education planning. The close cooperation between the Ministry of Education, Culture and Human Resources and the Ministry of Finance and Economic Empowerment was testimony to this.

In South Africa, the institutional structures for the coordination of economic and education policy existed in, for example, the Presidency's Policy Unit and in the National Planning Commission that was established in late 2009. Policy documents such as the *Human Resource Development Strategy for South Africa*, the *Accelerated and Shared Growth Initiative for South Africa* and *Industrial Policy Action Plan* had also taken up the need for coordination between the two sectors. Moreover, the higher education institutional funding policy provided incentives for institutions to produce more PhDs and reward peer-reviewed publications.

In Kenya there was evidence of a degree of cooperation between the Ministry of Higher Education, Science and Technology and the President's Office, which was responsible for the design and implementation of the country's major policy document, namely *Kenya Vision 2030*. However, there was little evidence of explicit economic and education planning. **>>**

BOX 3 continued ...

Coordination and consensus-building of government agencies in higher education

In Mauritius, there was evidence of consensus-building in higher education between the Ministry of Tertiary Education, Science, Research and Technology, the Tertiary Education Commission and higher education institutions. However, this appeared to be intermittent and taking place in the absence of specific forums for this purpose. In South Africa a specific forum, Higher Education South Africa, had been established for coordination and consensus-building between the Department of Higher Education and Training and universities. Former President Mbeki also created a Higher Education Working Group primarily to assess the role that universities could play in the country's development. In Kenya, there was some evidence of informal collaboration between government, universities and donors on higher education goals and implementation.

Structures linking universities and governments: The national commissions

All of the eight countries had regulatory bodies (called councils or commissions of higher or tertiary education) that constituted the link between higher education institutions and the government. However, the effectiveness of these institutions varied in terms of their regulatory and other functions. In Mozambique and Tanzania, it was not possible, on the basis of available information, to comment on the effectiveness of their regulatory bodies, namely the National Council for Higher Education and the Commission for Universities, respectively. In Uganda, the National Council for Higher Education appeared to be regulating public universities and undertaking appropriate research. In Mauritius and Botswana, the Councils appeared to be relatively influential in policy-making and regulation. In both Ghana and Mauritius, they played a prominent role in institutional funding. In Kenya, the commission appeared to be relatively weak in relation to its role and responsibilities vis-à-vis public universities, but appeared to be playing a much more appropriate role with respect to private universities. In South Africa, the Council on Higher Education was supposed to play both an advisory policy role to the ministry and act as a qualification regulator. In practice, however, it was the latter role in which it had been most active.

FINDINGS

- At the national level, there were considerable coordination activities in most countries, ranging from forums to clusters and the reorganisation of national ministries. However, this was mostly weak or 'symbolic' coordination.
- There were certainly many tight networks between government officials and university leadership, but it seems these were more orientated towards political connections.
- In all the countries, tertiary or higher education councils had been established, partially to compensate for weak ministries, and also to do 'independent' certification and quality assessments. At the time of the study, they were all undergoing 'role redefinitions', but could become key players in coordination and implementation monitoring.

Implementation

Table 7 summarises the ratings of the implementation indicators for the eight countries and universities (see Table C2 in Appendix C for an elaboration of these indicators).

TABLE 7 Implementation of knowledge policies and activities

Indicators	Max. score	Botswana	Ghana	Kenya	Mauritius	Moz.	South Africa	Tanzania	Uganda
NATIONAL LEVEL	12	8	8	8	8	5	11	7	6
Role of the ministry responsible for higher education	3	2	2	2	2	1	2	2	1
Implementation to 'steer' higher education towards development	3	2	1	1	2	1	3	2	1
Balance/ratio of sources of income for institutions	3	2	3	3	2	1	3	1	2
Funding consistency	3	2	2	2	2	2	3	2	2
UNIVERSITY LEVEL	18	10	8	8	13	7	13	10	10
Specific units, funding or appointments linked to economic development	3	1	1	1	3	1	1	1	1
Incentives and rewards for development-related activities	3	2	1	2	1	2	2	1	2
Teaching programmes linked to the labour market	3	3	2	1	2	1	3	2	2
Special programmes linking students to economic development	3	1	1	2	3	1	2	3	1
Research activities becoming more economy-oriented	3	2	2	1	3	1	2	2	3
Levels of government and institutional funding for research	3	1	1	1	1	1	3	1	1
TOTALS	30	18	16	16	21	12	24	17	16

South Africa was the only country with steering capacity, a stable funding regime and a sustainable ratio of sources of income. However, it did not have a vision of the role of higher education in development, meaning that steering was mainly based on dealing with issues internal to the higher education system. The two systems that appeared to have the most serious national-level capacity problems were Uganda and Mozambique, with the latter being de-capacitated by the dissolution of the Ministry of Higher Education, Science and Technology.

In a number of countries the government subsidy system was not only unstable, it also discouraged enterprising behaviour through a system that 'penalised' institutions for raising third-stream income by subtracting the amounts raised from the following year's government subsidy.

BOX 4

IMPLEMENTATION OF KNOWLEDGE POLICIES AND ACTIVITIES

South Africa rated 'strong' on three implementation indicators: Implementation to 'steer' higher education towards development; balance/ratio of sources of income for institutions; and funding consistency. South Africa used the institutional funding formula to steer the system by providing incentives for doctoral study and publications. The university funding system was diversified between government provision, tuition fees and institutional own income. Finally, the country provided a good practice model of consistency in funding based on higher education institutional plans, government budget constraints, and the medium term expenditure framework.

Ghana and Kenya rated high on the indicator balance/ratio of sources of income for institutions. In the case of Ghana, there was evidence of attempts at both funding innovation and diversification of institutional funding sources. In the case of the former, a percentage of value-added tax was used to fund higher education capital expenditure, student loans and research. With regard to the latter, student fees were rising relative to government funding. Kenya (as well as Uganda) had developed a dual-track tuition-fee scheme to address the challenge of declining state funding. The scheme, which was highly inequitable, provided free education for a specific number of students who produced the best results in the school-leaving examinations, and charged fees to everybody else who was admitted. The inequity stems partly from the fact that most of those who got the full scholarships also attended the best schools in the country, and most often came from the richest households.

Implementation at the university level refers to units or structures linked to economic development, incentives for such activities, funding available, special programmes linked to the labour market and research activities that were economy-orientated (Box 5).

Of the eight universities in the sample, Mauritius was the only one with a number of specific structures and appointments linking the institution's activities to economic development. Most of these were focused on research, innovation and technology, as well as support for small and medium enterprises (SMEs). Mauritius also had a well-established focus on work-based learning, and a strong focus on economic development in its research and innovation clusters.

Interestingly, although NMMU had a low knowledge economy score (Table 1), it scored high on the implementation ratings. The university had set targets for enrolments in fields considered to be of high economic relevance and, of all the eight universities, had the highest level of research funding from both government and the institution. There were also moves towards the introduction of special programmes linking students to the labour market, and towards introducing an economic development focus into research agendas.

In the other universities, evidence of structures, appointments or funding for activities linked to economic development was only to be found in specific pockets in the institution.

While many of the universities had some form of incentive for academics to engage in research (e.g. Makerere), none of the universities incentivised their academic staff to engage in (economic) development-related research or teaching per se. At NMMU, there were (financial) incentives for academics to get involved in innovation but there were no incentives to get involved in other forms of engagement activities (e.g. community service or outreach), in terms of funding or time allocation. There were plans to develop a policy on the recognition and reward of research, teaching and engagement activities as well as the development of a workload policy that would ensure an appropriate balance between teaching, research and community engagement responsibilities.

BOX 5

IMPLEMENTATION OF KNOWLEDGE POLICIES AT UNIVERSITY LEVEL

Specific units, funding or appointments linked to economic development

Over the years, the University of Mauritius had established a number of posts and structures linked to furthering the institution's activities in relation to economic development:

- The Office of the Pro Vice-Chancellor for Research, Consultancy and Innovation, which managed and provided facilities and funding for all research, innovation and consultancy activities in the institution.

- The Consultancy and Contract Research Centre which coordinated all consultancy and contract research between the university and government, industry and other stakeholders.

- The Technology Management Group, which liaised between the university and external companies around research collaboration and the commercialisation of results.

- The Excellence Park with Multidisciplinary Centres of Excellence, the aim of which was to address national priorities and opportunities through promoting research and development.

- The University Support Network for Small and Medium Enterprises, which aimed to utilise university resources to contribute to the development and enhancement of SMEs, in line with the government's policy for promoting the sector.

Special programmes linking students to economic development

In recent years there had been increased emphasis at the University of Dar es Salaam on entrepreneurial training and small business development, in response to changes in the economy and wider business environment. The university had a policy on entrepreneurship which required that every student was exposed to entrepreneurship training. While some faculties and colleges offered a separate entrepreneurship course, others had mainstreamed entrepreneurship into their programmes. A Postgraduate Diploma and a Masters programme in Entrepreneurship and Enterprise Development had also been introduced. >>

Box 5 continued...

In partnership with the University of Bradford, the University of Mauritius was awarded a grant from the England-Africa Partnerships in Higher Education project of the British Council to incorporate work-based learning into the undergraduate curricula and to support work placements for undergraduate students to improve their employability. The Work-Based Learning Unit identified and trained mentors from industry who provided guidance and support to students during their work placements. These mentors also assessed the students on a range of competencies including communication, team work, improving own learning and performance, solving problems, working and applying numbers, using information technology and developing professionalism.

Teaching programmes linked to the labour market

In 2006, the national Department of Education in South Africa required NMMU to identify five academic growth areas as part of its Institutional Operational Plan and enrolment plan for the period 2006-2010. The university consulted a wide range of national policy documents and economic growth strategies in order to identify the five priority areas which included: infrastructure development; environmental and natural resource management; economic and business development; community and health development; and education, culture and communication.

The University of Botswana's strategic plan highlighted specific targets for undergraduate enrolments at the discipline level (following the *Student Enrolment Projections to 2016* report, published in 2008). The targets for 2016 included:

- Business and Information and Communication Technology 20%;
- Science, Engineering and Health Sciences 30%;
- Humanities and Social Sciences 31%; and
- Education 19%.

Research activities are becoming more economy-oriented

The University of Botswana had identified a number of priority research themes based on existing areas of research strength, national research priorities, international research trends, and emerging social needs. This institutional research agenda included a direct economic development focus in the economic diversification and entrepreneurship theme, as well as an indirect focus in other themes linked to sustainable development and poverty reduction.

Makerere University had an institutional research agenda which was driven by the university and its researchers, by national priorities and, at times, by the agendas of foreign donors. The multidisciplinary research agenda was informed by the government's *Poverty Eradication Action Plan*. An economic development focus was inherent, albeit indirectly, in most of the themes, such as: education for development; food and nutrition; sustainable environment development; natural resources utilisation and conservation; and cross-cutting themes such as appropriate technology, economics and bio-technology.

The University of Mauritius' *Strategic Research and Innovation Framework* outlined a number of priority clusters for research and innovation activities. A number of these included an economic development focus, such as those relating to science and technology and to transforming the Mauritian economy, while others had an indirect focus as they related to health and the environment.

FINDINGS

- At the national level one of the weakest aspects of linking higher education to economic development was implementation: most ministries of education did not have steering instruments or mechanisms.
- Some ministries disincentivised institutions from generating third-stream income.
- Every university had at least one development-related structure and one or more special programme/s. The problem is that in too many cases these initiatives are driven by individuals rather than being institutionalised. In addition, these special implementation efforts need to be more connected.
- Despite policies that extol the importance of research related to development activities (mainly through focus themes), few institutions had special funds for this. Neither was research related to development rewarded through incentives beyond the traditional academic promotion system.

4.2   University connectedness to external stakeholders

Industry and community

Most of the universities in the sample talked about the importance of engaging with external stakeholders in their institutional plans or research policies. Indeed, in all of the universities there was evidence of such engagement through their teaching, research, consultancy and other forms of 'service' activities. A review of a selection of development-related activities in the eight universities (see section 4.3) indicates that a wide range of external stakeholders stood to benefit from the teaching, research and service undertaken by academics – from government, foreign donors, industry, the private sector and non-governmental organisations (NGOs) to fishers, small-scale farmers, street traders and people living with disease burdens. Universities also collaborated with or undertook work on behalf of a range of external stakeholders, especially government, industry, the private sector, and non-governmental or community-based organisations.

While these linkages were not a key focus of this study, we did gather some evidence on the nature and extent of the universities' interactions with the key external stakeholders during the interviews – in particular with industry and the private sector (including SMEs), and foreign donors (section 4.2).

While there was evidence of linkages with industry and the private sector in all eight universities, this was generally confined to the level of units or centres rather than institutional-level partnerships or linkages. In addition, except for ad hoc consultancies at NMMU and Mauritius, there was hardly any evidence of university engagement in research and development (R&D) with or for industry. To a large extent this is because the industrial sector in most of these countries is under-developed, and because there is very limited private sector R&D – where global companies do have operations in African countries, their R&D is usually undertaken elsewhere. Of course, this is a problem in most developing countries but it is particularly acute in Africa. Some of the universities were beginning to address the lack of interaction between their institutions and industry or the private sector through the establishment of university–industry liaison offices (e.g. Mauritius). Some interviewees suggested that part of the problem was also the attitudes of academics, some of whom are unwilling to engage with external stakeholders.

Evidence of interaction with the private sector took two forms. The first was in the area of education and training. Examples included the use of people from the private sector on advisory committees responsible for curricula design and revision (Mauritius and Botswana); work placements; and for specific, customised training programmes. The second and most prevalent form of interaction was business development and support for SMEs. Examples included: the business incubator projects or units at Mauritius and Dar es Salaam; the Automotive Components Technology Station at NMMU; the Innovation Systems and Clusters Programme in Eastern Africa operating at Eduardo Mondlane, Dar es Salaam and Makerere; the Uganda Gatsby Trust at Makerere; the University of Botswana Business Clinic; and, the African Clothing and Footwear Research Network at Nairobi.

Only two of the universities – Nairobi and Mauritius – had units dedicated to coordinating the activities with external stakeholders (Box 6).

BOX 6

UNIVERSITY CONNECTEDNESS TO EXTERNAL GROUPINGS

External stakeholders involved in curriculum design

At the University of Mauritius, faculties and departments were required to engage advisory committees, which included external stakeholders from the public and private sectors and NGOs, around the development of new academic programmes and revisions to curricula. At the University of Botswana, every department had an advisory board which informed curriculum development. These boards comprise members of the department as well as key stakeholders from outside of the university (e.g. government, the private sector and NGOs).

Coordination of consultancy and other engagement activities

The University of Nairobi Enterprises and Services (UNES) Ltd was established in 1996 with the aim of promoting and coordinating the various income-generating activities of the university, including teaching, research and consultancy activities. UNES was registered as a private company, limited by shares, and operated as a separate legal entity, independent of the university. Amongst others, UNES was responsible for promoting, coordinating and providing managerial services for income-generating activities within the university.

The key unit in the University of Mauritius for coordinating linkages and activities with government and industry was the Centre for Consultancy and Contract Research. The centre aimed to encourage and facilitate consultancy activities amongst staff as a way of contributing to the socio-economic development of the country. It coordinated all consultancy and contract research, and managed intellectual property generated by university research, licensing and technology transfers. The centre's Consultancy Watch Unit was established in 2006 to assist staff to identify and develop consultancy opportunities.

FINDINGS

- While there was evidence of connectedness between the university and industry or the private sector in all eight universities, this was generally confined to the level of units or centres rather than institutional-level partnerships.
- Except for ad hoc consultancies at NMMU and Mauritius, there was hardly any evidence of university engagement in R&D with, or for, industry.

Foreign donors

Development aid contributed to the development of post-independence universities in Africa. However, aid diminished dramatically during the 1980s and 1990s following the World Bank policy shift to primary education, and as relations between governments and universities deteriorated.

Development aid to higher education in Africa picked up again significantly in the post-2000 period. The CHET development aid study (Maassen *et al.* 2007) estimated that about USD 1 billion was donated to higher education in Africa during the 2000–2005 period. This new interest was considerably strengthened at the G8 Gleneagles summit (July 2005) where Africa and the Millennium Development Goals were the major focus. Following the summit, the office of the British prime minister issued a communiqué proclaiming an 'historic opportunity' and 'a renewed commitment': 'This is a moment of opportunity for Africa. Its leaders have embraced a new vision for the continent's future which recognises their leading role in addressing the continent's challenges and realising its opportunities' (G8 Gleneagles 2005: 11). The prime minister urged a focus on Africa because it 'is the only continent not on track to meet any of the goals of the Millennium Declaration by 2015' (ibid.).

The summit made a pledge to increase annual Official Development Assistance to Africa by USD 22.6 billion by 2010. As the G8 accounts for 70% of all Official Development Assistance spending, this increase would more than double G8 aid to Africa. Specific goals included massive investments in education, and HIV and poverty reduction, which could have constituted a major push towards achieving the Millennium Development Goals.

According to an independent assessment of the G8 'promises to Africa' (Gastfriend & Morton 2010), 'the G8 is on track to deliver 61% of the Gleneagles commitments by 2010, an increase of approximately USD 13.7 billion per year [of the 22.6 billion promised]. The bulk of the shortfall falls on three countries: France, Germany and Italy', while 'by the end of 2010 Japan, the US and Canada will have exceeded their commitments' and the UK is expected to almost fulfil its promises. So, while not living up to the ambitious pledge of 2005, substantial amounts of funds are going into development aid, and there is a renewed interest in higher education.

A reading of the main international declarations and agreements on development aid in Africa shows widely divergent approaches, with no generally accepted 'development model' or approach that links a set of key drivers for development. This is probably owing to the particularity of the national interests of the participating countries. But, in Africa, there is also no agreement on the role of higher education in development aid. For example, the Economic Commission for Africa produced a weighty tome in 2004 entitled *Economic Report on Africa – Unlocking Africa's trade potential*. There is no reference in this highly publicised document regarding the role of higher education and its importance for knowledge creation, skills development and development in general (Maassen *et al.* 2007). A similar lack of focus on higher education characterises the official documents of the New Partnership for Africa's Development (NEPAD) and the Southern African Development Community.

Even if the G8 has only managed to meet 61% of its target, it still amounts to a substantial increase in development aid to Africa in general, and to higher education in particular, and to significant amounts of funds. The issue is thus not only about more aid, but importantly how to spend the aid more effectively. In the context of this study, our interest in the relationship between foreign aid and higher education in Africa has three dimensions. These include agenda-setting, the coordination of aid projects, and the possible effects of development aid on the academic cores of African universities.

According to institutional leaders at the University of Dar es Salaam, not all donor agencies took the government's priorities into account, while others did. The Swedish International Development Cooperation Agency (SIDA) was mentioned as a particular example of a big donor that responds to proposals from local demand. Some interviewees suggested that donors were more likely to push their own agendas with individual academics. For example, one respondent said that 'there are those donors who have special agendas and they will always go to a particular member of staff or a particular head of department'.

At the University of Ghana, a number of respondents spoke about the tensions between responding to the agendas of foreign donors in order to secure research or project funding, on the one hand, and addressing local needs, on the other. For example, one project leader talked about the difficulties of raising funds for new health problems such as chronic high blood pressure, heart disease and diabetes when donors only wanted to fund research into tropical (malaria) and infectious (HIV/Aids) diseases. Another highlighted the tension between donor and country priorities, as well as traditional forms of academic assessment.

Some senior academics also commented on the changing of, and increasing lack of clarity about, what donors wanted to fund, particularly in the social sciences. In the words of a senior academic at the University of Nairobi: 'I'm not sure I know what the donors are interested in. I don't mind ideology, even if I don't agree with it, at least I know where I stand, but with many of the major donors I don't know anymore where I stand – for the life of me I don't know who is funding the social sciences.'

Coordination of agendas and projects was a major problem, not to mention the considerable administrative effort required for accounting to multiple donors. At some institutions the data collected and formatted for donor reports were much more systematic and organised than the data for government or institutional management.

Two universities where considerable effort and resources had been put into donor coordination were Dar es Salaam and Eduardo Mondlane (Box 7). According to the Director of Planning and Finance at Dar es Salaam, they were trying to move towards institutionalising the strategic plan in terms of foreign donor funding that comes into the university. This was only beginning to be possible since, in the past, the institution's needs were so many that they would accept any money that was offered:

> *You know, when you have so many needs – we have deteriorating students'
> hostels, we don't have enough teaching facilities, the laboratories are dead, the
> workshops are dead. You see, wherever you get funds you tend to say: yes,
> please give me because I'm in need of this. But I think now given what we have
> received in terms of a loan from the World Bank support, we can now say: …
> these are the areas that we now need support, in the next five years.*

The director also reported that while there was some coordination between donor agencies at a national level (e.g. where donors were aware of what other donors were funding at the government level), there was no coordination in terms of what was being funded in the university (as the money was channelled via the national treasury):

> *It was very interesting to see, with just two more partners we could see already
> there was no coordination. They didn't know each other and they were over-
> lapping some activities. So it made us realise that it's very urgent and important
> to have this horizontal dialogue, not just vertical dialogue. I mean, the donors
> communicate with us but they don't communicate with each other.*

At Eduardo Mondlane, the newly established Donor Coordination Unit, which reported directly to the vice-chancellor, was responsible for coordinating institutional and foreign donor interests and agendas. This unit emerged out of the long-standing unit responsible for coordination of the SIDA/SAREC[15] cooperation. The unit at Eduardo Mondlane would also be responsible for bringing together major donors to meet and discuss their activities in order to coordinate funding areas and reporting mechanisms, and to avoid duplication or overlap where possible. However, the unit's coordinator reported that at a recent meeting of large donors, it was evident that there was little coordination between them in terms of funding areas and activities. In addition, it was virtually impossible to ensure coordination with the smaller donor-funded projects since these were usually negotiated with individual researchers.

Eduardo Mondlane University, which received the largest proportion of donor aid amongst the universities in our sample, has had a relationship with SIDA/SAREC for more than 30

---

15   SAREC is the Department for Research Cooperation of SIDA.

years. It has also received large development grants from the World Bank via the government. Over this period, SIDA/SAREC has funded individual projects, capacity development (including masters and PhD degrees), bigger research programmes and a facilities fund which covers expensive equipment and the maintenance of laboratories and so on. Over the past few years, it has been mandatory to include masters and PhD training in the larger research programmes funded by SIDA.

However, although there has been an increase in enrolments in masters programmes at Eduardo, their doctoral enrolments were the weakest in the sample of eight countries (Table 3). This is partially due to the fact that many doctoral candidates still enrol at overseas universities, particularly in the donor countries, but more importantly because there is no coordinated triangle of government, university and donor support. Government has abdicated the contribution to research and doctoral training to donors. But donors cannot be a 'surrogate state': training at the highest level and knowledge production at a globally competitive level requires concentrated effort from the government, donors and the university.

BOX 7

CONNECTING INTERNAL UNIVERSITY AND EXTERNAL DONOR INTERESTS

At Eduardo Mondlane University, the Donor Coordination Unit, which reported directly to the vice-chancellor, was responsible for coordinating institutional and foreign donor interests and agendas. This included negotiating with the larger donors that the programmes funded were aligned with both institutional and national priorities. The unit would also be responsible for bringing major donors together to discuss their activities with a view to coordinating funding areas and reporting mechanisms.

The key coordinating body at the University of Dar es Salaam was the Department of Planning and Finance. The department coordinated planning and implementation of the strategic plan in various units, raised funds from different sources, and oversaw the income and expenditure on these funds. Of particular interest to this study is the department's role in ensuring a degree of alignment between the institution's strategic objectives, academic activities and foreign donor interests.

FINDINGS

- The coordination of agendas and projects with donors was a major problem, not to mention the considerable administrative effort required for accounting to multiple donors. Only two universities (Dar es Salaam and Eduardo Mondlane) had established strong coordination structures.
- Particularly amongst social scientists there was a perception of a decrease in donor interest, and an increasing lack of clarity about what donors want to fund.

4.3   The connectedness of development activities to the academic core

A key issue for the relationship between higher education and economic development is to establish a *productive* relationship between knowledge and connectedness. On the one hand, if there is an overemphasis on the basic knowledge activities of teaching and research – in other words, an excessive inward orientation towards strengthening the academic core – this results in the university becoming an 'ivory tower'. Or, if the academic core is weak, an overemphasis on knowledge results in the 'ancillary' role of the university (i.e. no direct role in development). On the other hand, an overemphasis in the university on connecting to development activities weakens the academic core and the university has little new or relevant knowledge to offer in the exchange relationship.

The challenge for universities, then, is to deal with this inherent tension between 'buffering' (protecting) the core technologies of the institution, and 'bridging' (linking) those with external actors (Scott 2001: 199–211). In reality, the boundaries between internal and external are not that clear cut. A number of higher education experts, such as Gibbons *et al.* (1994) and Scott (2001), have argued that with globalisation and its associated 'new' forms of knowledge production, the boundaries are becoming increasingly blurred and permeable.

The higher education studies literature describes this problem in terms of the conceptual notion of 'coupling' (Scott 2001; Weick 1976); that is, the extent to which the core and the external (or 'periphery') are linked with, or connected to, one another. In 'tight coupling', the boundary is weak and the university is in a direct, 'instrumental' relationship with external actors such as government or industry. In 'loose-coupling', the boundary is stronger, such as in the traditional notion of the university as a self-governing institution, which assumes an indirect contribution to development. The more complex relationship is with the 'engine of development' notion where there are multiple, simultaneous forms of knowledge production and exchange.

For the purposes of this study, we used the term 'connectedness' to refer to the relationship (and tension) between the inward focus on strengthening and maintaining the academic core, and the outward focus on linking with external stakeholders and development. In this section, we present a methodology for investigating this tension and apply this methodology to a small selection of projects from the eight universities in the study.

We begin with a brief overview of the methodology employed in collecting and analysing the data in order to address these questions.

Methodology

In preparation for the research team's visit to each institution, institutional leaders were asked to identify five to ten development-related projects (i.e. with an economic development or poverty reduction focus) to include in the investigation. In the end, detailed information was gathered on 44 projects and centres across the eight universities. While these projects and centres might not necessarily constitute 'flagship' or 'exemplary' projects in every case, they were considered by university leadership to be strongly connected to development.

We operationalised 'connectedness' along two dimensions. The first dimension is 'articulation' which has a number of aspects. Firstly, it refers to the extent to which the aims and outcomes of development-related activities articulate with national development priorities and the university's strategic objectives. Secondly, it refers to the linkages the project has with two of the groups of stakeholders in the triangle – the government (usually through specific government departments or agencies) and external stakeholders (e.g. industry, small businesses, NGOs or community groups such as fishers or small-scale farmers). In particular, our focus is on the extent to which there are linkages with an 'implementation agency' (i.e. an external body which takes up the knowledge and/or its products generated or applied through research or training). Thirdly, articulation takes into account linkages generated through sources of funding in two respects: whether the project/centre obtains funding from one or more of the three stakeholder groups (government, an external funder or the university itself); and the extent to which the project/centre develops a relationship with its funders over time. This latter aspect is determined through the nature of the financial sustainability of the project.

The second dimension focuses on the extent to which development activities serve to 'strengthen the academic core' of the university. This was operationalised in terms of the extent to which the work undertaken in projects/centres feeds into teaching or curriculum development; is linked to the formal training of students; enables academics to publish in academic publications (journals, books, etc.); is linked to international academic networks; and generates new knowledge (versus applying existing knowledge).

These various aspects relating to 'articulation' and 'strengthening the academic core' were converted into indicators (Table 9) which could then be applied to an analysis of the development-related projects and centres included in the study. On the basis of the indicator ratings, the projects/centres were plotted on a graph depicting the intersection between 'articulation' and 'strengthening the academic core'. Detailed descriptions and analyses of the 44 projects/centres can be found in the eight case study reports which are available on the CHET website.

The project data and analysis

For the purposes of this synthesis discussion, one project or centre from each of the eight universities was selected for analysis and discussion. Together, these projects/centres represent the spectrum of different types or categories, such as long-term research programmes or short-term consultancies, institutionalised training and small business support. Table 8 provides an overview of the eight projects/centres. Table 9 provides the summary 'articulation' and 'strengthening the academic core' ratings, respectively. The projects/centres are then plotted along the two axes in Figure 3.

TABLE 8 Overview of the development-related projects/centres

University	Project/centre	Classification	Time frame	Funder(s)	Beneficiaries	Initiation/agenda-setting	Economic development focus
Botswana	UB Business Clinic (BC)	Practical training and support services	1995, ongoing	University, income generated through student businesses	Students and the public who want to start or grow their SMEs	Faculty staff	Support to establish new, or grow existing, SMEs
Dar es Salaam	SME Gatsby Clubs (SMEGC)	Small business support	2004, ongoing	Foreign donors, the university	SMEs in Tanzania	Staff in the university	Training, support and facilities to SMEs in target groups
Eduardo Mondlane	Energy, Environment and Climate Change (EECC)	Research programme	2006, ongoing	Foreign donors, government agency	Government, private sector, NGOs, students, people living in rural areas	Academic staff	Development of renewable energy solutions
Ghana	Noguchi Memorial Institute for Medical Research (NMIMR)	Research institute and postgraduate training programmes	1979, ongoing	Foreign donors, government	People of Ghana, government health agencies, local NGOs	Foreign donors, institute staff	Research, training and diagnostic services for the public health sector
Makerere	Community-Based Education and Service provision (COBES)	Community-based education and service provision	2003/2004, ongoing	Foreign donors, the university, some income generation	College of Health Sciences students, local communities	University staff	Healthcare provision to poor and rural communities
Mauritius	Review of Strategies for Poverty Alleviation (RPAS)	Externally-funded consultancy	February–October 2009	Independent consultative body to government	Government ministry	Consultative body	Inform policy-making and build capacity amongst stakeholders involved in poverty alleviation
Nairobi	African Collaborative Centre for Earth System Science (ACCESS)	Long-term research and capacity building programme	1989, ongoing	Government agency, the university, foreign donors	African science and policy communities, NGOs, local communities	University academic, international academic network	Research and capacity building around environmental issues that are linked to poverty
NMMU	Automotive Components Technology Station (ACTS)	Consultancy projects and training	2002, ongoing	Government agency, income generation	SMEs in the automotive components industry	Academics with industry experience, industry donor	Consultancy projects and training for industry (especially SMEs)

TABLE 9 Development projects/centres: 'Articulation' and 'strengthening the academic core' ratings

Projects/centres	UB Business Clinic	SME Gatsby Clubs	Energy, Environment and Climate Change	Noguchi Memorial Institute for Medical Research	Community-Based Education and Service	Review of Strategies for Poverty Alleviation	African Collaborative Centre for Earth System Science	Automotive Components Technology Station
ARTICULATION RATING (maximum score = 13)								
Institutional objectives	2	2	0	0	0	0	0	2
National priorities	1	2	2	2	1	2	1	2
Number of funding source(s)	2	2	2	2	3	1	3	2
Funding sustainability	3	2	2	3	2	1	3	3
Implementation agency	0	2	1	2	0	1	1	2
Total articulation rating	**8**	**10**	**7**	**9**	**6**	**5**	**8**	**11**
STRENGTHENING ACADEMIC CORE RATING (maximum score = 5)								
Teaching/curriculum development	0	0	1	1	1	1	1	1
Formal training of students	0	1	1	1	1	0	1	1
Generate new knowledge	0	0	1	1	0	1	1	1
Academic publications	0	0	1	1	1	0	1	1
Link to international academic networks	0	0	1	1	0	0	1	1
Total academic core rating	**0**	**1**	**5**	**5**	**3**	**2**	**5**	**5**

'Articulation' key:
- **Institutional objectives/National priorities:**
  2 = Direct (link to specific strategic objective or national priority)
  1 = Indirect (broad/general reference)
  0 = None (no reported link)
- **Number of funding sources:**
  1 for each of the following: University; Government; Foreign donor; Income generation
- **Funding sustainability:**
  1 = Once-off, short-term (a project that is one year or less in duration and which receives only one round of funding)
  2 = Long-term but capped (a project that is more than one year in duration and which receives one or more rounds of funding, but the funding is capped)
  3 = Ongoing (a project which receives ongoing funding, e.g. from the university or from income generation)
- **Link to implementation agency:**
  2 = Direct
  1 = Indirect
  0 = None

'Strengthening the academic core' key: 1 = Yes 0 = No

FIGURE 3 Plotting the development activities

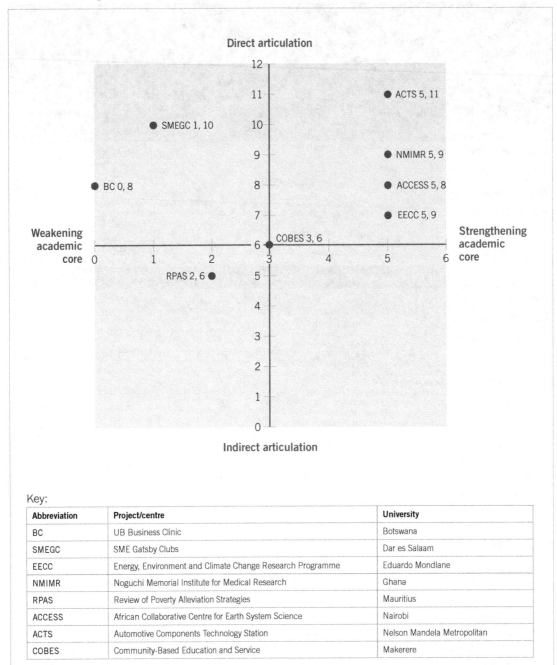

Key:

Abbreviation	Project/centre	University
BC	UB Business Clinic	Botswana
SMEGC	SME Gatsby Clubs	Dar es Salaam
EECC	Energy, Environment and Climate Change Research Programme	Eduardo Mondlane
NMIMR	Noguchi Memorial Institute for Medical Research	Ghana
RPAS	Review of Poverty Alleviation Strategies	Mauritius
ACCESS	African Collaborative Centre for Earth System Science	Nairobi
ACTS	Automotive Components Technology Station	Nelson Mandela Metropolitan
COBES	Community-Based Education and Service	Makerere

Discussion

In terms of our analysis, which focused on the interaction between the articulation of these projects with external stakeholders and strengthening the academic core of the institution, the projects/centres fell into three groups (see Figure 3).

The first group were those which fall within the top right-hand quadrant of the graph, which indicates that they scored strongly on both the articulation and academic core axes. There were examples of such projects/centres in all eight universities in the study. In practice, this means that these projects/centres had found a way of balancing the potential tensions between the two objectives of articulating to external stakeholders whilst also strengthening the core knowledge activities of the institution. On the one hand, projects/centres such as the Automotive Components Technology Station, the Noguchi Memorial Institute for Medical Research (NMIMR), the African Collaborative Centre for Earth System Science (ACCESS) and the Energy, Environment and Climate Change Research Programme reflected specific national development priorities in their aims and objectives; had more than one funding source and plans for financial sustainability; and had links to one or more implementation agencies. On the other hand, the work of these projects/centres provided opportunities for the formal training of students, fed into teaching and curriculum development, generated new knowledge and academic publications, and had linkages to international academic networks.

A second group of projects/centres are those which fall somewhere within the middle of the graph, indicating that while they are connected to external stakeholders in some respects, and go some way towards strengthening the academic core, they are not strong on either. The example in the selected projects above is the Community-Based Education and Service.

The third group, which contains the smallest number of projects/centres, mostly falls within the top-left quadrant of the graph. These projects/centres were often well-connected to external stakeholders via funding or implementation agencies, but they score poorly on the academic core axis, meaning that although they were making a contribution to development, they were not strengthening the core knowledge activities of the university. Amongst the selected projects highlighted above, the three examples of this included UB Business Clinic, the SME Gatsby Clubs and the short-term consultancy project on Reviewing Poverty Alleviation Strategies – all of which were disconnected from the academic core.

The first observation is that these projects/centres were chosen by the institutional leadership as cases of their university's contribution to development. What we could not ascertain, owing to a lack of information, was how many short-term consultancy projects there were and how connected/disconnected these were to development goals and the strengthening of the academic core. Doing an in-depth case study of a sample of institutions would be very illuminating in this regard.

The second observation is that the projects/centres which scored high on articulation and strengthening the academic core are world-class. To mention two: ACCESS at the University of Nairobi is a multi-funded centre of excellence that plays a significant role in the United Nations Framework Convention on Climate Change, while having postgraduate students and fellows from all over the world. The NMIMR in Ghana, co-funded by the Japanese government for 30 years, is a leading biomedical research and training centre in communicable diseases that also performs national health laboratory services. In terms of sustainability, the only difference between the two centres is that the NMIMR is very institutionalised, with successive directors coming from the faculty, while ACCESS seems much more dependent on one exceptional individual. The problem in our sample is that there were simply not enough of these activities that were connected to both development goals and the academic core.

FINDINGS

- Projects/centres that were considered by university leadership to be strongly connected to development tended to score well on the articulation indicators – in other words, they reflected national priorities (and to a lesser extent institutional objectives), had more than one funding source and, in some cases, plans for financial sustainability, and may have had a connection to an implementation agency.
- A number of these projects/centres also managed to keep a strong connection with the academic core of the university, whilst others were almost entirely disconnected from these core knowledge activities.
- At each of the universities there were 'exemplary' development projects/centres. The problem was scale: there were simply not enough, and some seemed overly-dependent on exceptional individuals.

Part 3
KEY FINDINGS FROM THE EIGHT AFRICAN CASE STUDIES

In this section we present the key findings from the eight national and institutional case studies undertaken in 2009/2010 which included:

· Botswana and the University of Botswana
· Ghana and the University of Ghana
· Kenya and the University of Nairobi
· Mauritius and the University of Mauritius
· Mozambique and the Eduardo Mondlane University
· South Africa and the Nelson Mandela Metropolitan University
· Tanzania and the University of Dar es Salaam, and
· Uganda and Makerere University.

The key findings address the following questions:

· How does each country fare on the macro higher education and economic development preconditions for an effective and productive relationship between higher education and economic development that were identified in the international case studies? (See Pillay 2010b and section 1.4.)
· To what extent is there a pact between key stakeholders (national and institutional) about the role of higher education in general, and in relation to economic development in particular?
· Do the individual universities in the sample have capacity to make a contribution to economic development in terms of (a) the nature and strength of their academic core, and (b) the connectedness of the development-related activities to the academic core?

The concepts and theories referred to in this section are outlined in greater detail in Part 2.

5

Botswana and the University of Botswana

5.1 The higher education and economic development context in Botswana

How did Botswana fare in meeting the 'preconditions' for an effective and productive relationship between higher education and economic development identified by Pillay's (2010b) investigation of three successful systems?

High-quality schooling: While participation rates in primary and secondary education were relatively high, the evidence suggested that there was still a long way to go to achieving universally high quality of provision and outcomes in the schooling system. There was some evidence also that the drop-out rates throughout the different phases of schooling were high with the result that a relatively small proportion of the relevant age-cohort was able to access higher education. Improving quality of schooling must therefore be a priority for policy-makers in order to ensure the development of a more 'successful' (i.e. vis-à-vis development) higher education system.

Effective economic and education planning: The government had produced a number of impressive planning documents including *Botswana Vision 2016* and the National Development Plans. In all of these, the role of education is stressed, particularly that of higher education, if Botswana is to become a player in both the globalising world and knowledge economy. However, much more needs to be done around indicative planning in both sectors to ensure that:

- The higher education sector is able to produce appropriate human capital outcomes through its education and training function, and technology through its research and innovation function; and
- The economy is able to productively use such higher education outputs to drive the country onto a higher growth path from the current one based on primary commodities.

Role of the state: The state in Botswana was playing a strong and innovative role in higher education especially with respect to the overall level of funding, human resource planning, and stimulating partnerships with the private sector, both with private higher education institutions, and in creating a public–private partnership leading to the establishment of the new university of technology. However, the state needs to consider whether it is using its limited financial resources in the most equitable, efficient and effective manner possible.

In this regard, consideration should be given to the introduction of more widespread cost sharing in public institutions.

Partnerships: There was evidence of partnerships between the state and the private sector (e.g. the new university of technology). However, it was not clear what role the state was playing in promoting industry–university partnerships around research and innovation, a key factor for enhanced economic development. Given the 'infant' nature of the Botswana economy (outside of diamonds) and its dependence on South Africa for manufactured goods and services, it may be necessary for the government to provide incentives to stimulate the start-up of such industry–university linkages around research and innovation.

Institutional differentiation: Given the small size of the public university sector, it was to be expected that there would be little functional differentiation and that the established University of Botswana would attempt to undertake its education and training, and research and innovation functions on as wide a front as possible. However, there were two other elements of differentiation, that is, between public and private institutions, and between universities and colleges. With respect to the former, it was evident that the private institutions were growing at a much faster rate in terms of enrolments. From an access point of view, this was encouraging as long as the Tertiary Education Council was ensuring that a high (or at least comparable) quality of education was being provided. With respect to the colleges, anecdotal evidence suggested that quality remained a huge challenge. Given that about half of the tertiary education student body attends these institutions, it raised important concerns about the ability of these institutions to produce human capital that was appropriately geared to contribute to economic growth and development.

Quality: Serious questions have been raised about the quality of teaching and learning across the higher education system. It was evident that serious efforts have to be made to improve quality of outputs emerging from the system to enable higher education to play a more clearly defined role in economic development.

Funding: State funding of higher education was in line with international benchmarks. However, questions can be raised on two fronts. First, it was evident that the system of state funding of students ostensibly through a combination of loans and grants may have been inefficient (with respect to poor recovery of loans) and ineffective (in attaining the desired graduate outcomes). Second, consideration should be given to the introduction of increased cost-sharing through more widely-spread use of tuition fees in public institutions.

Innovation: On a global scale, Botswana belongs to a large group of developing countries that are neither involved in science and technology innovation nor its diffusion at any significant level. The capacity to innovate and diffuse technology is a product of the quality of physical infrastructure; the state of education and educational attainment by the citizenry; the size and maturity of markets; as well as the level of integration into the world economy through trade and investment. Looking at Botswana's strong fiscal position, it has been argued that it meets the basic requirements for developing a strong science and technology capability and capacity. It has research institutions that are well resourced to carry out significant research, but outputs have to date not been reflective of this potential. Moreover, the state needs to define more clearly what the role of higher education institutions can and should be with respect to innovation.

5.2   Evidence of a pact around the role of higher education in Botswana?

Botswana's indicator ratings for the role of knowledge and universities in national and institutional policies and plans are presented in Table 10.

TABLE 10 **Role for knowledge and universities in development in Botswana**

National rating = 4/6			
The concept of a knowledge economy features in the national development plan	3 Strong Appears in a number of policies	**2 Weak** Only mentioned in one policy	1 Absent Not mentioned at all
A role for higher education in development in national policies and plans	3 Prevalent Clearly mentioned in development policies	**2 Weak**	1 Absent
University rating = 3/6			
Concept of a knowledge economy features in institutional policies and plans	3 Features strongly in strategic plan and/or research policy/ strategy	**2** Vague reference in strategic plan or research policy	1 Not mentioned at all
Institutional policies with regard to the university's role in economic development	3 Institutional policy	2 Embedded in strategic plan, research policy, etc.	**1** No formal policies

FINDINGS

- The education department, through the Botswana Tertiary Education Council, had a state-of-the-art knowledge economy policy, but it was not shared across other departments.
- There was no broad agreement that knowledge, and by implication higher education, is key to development.
- The reorganisation of the Tertiary Education Council and human resources department shows an emerging awareness about the importance of the knowledge economy approach.

Notions of the role of knowledge and universities in development

Table 11 summarises the notions of the role of higher education held by national and institutional stakeholders, and indicates whether the notion was strong, prevalent, present or absent altogether.

The University of Botswana stakeholders interviewed showed a very clear awareness of a shift from the traditional person power development role of the university to an orientation towards the production of knowledge. Very clearly articulated was that the university had a development role and, at least among leadership, there was no mention of an institutional approach, or any mention of autonomy and isolation. While the overall discourse was instrumental there was also a strong 'engagement' or service orientation, and at the leadership level the focus was on research, innovation and industry. However, even in the interviews it emerged that implementing this new development orientation was proving very difficult; at that stage, it was more on the level of aspiration, with very little implementation.

While acknowledging that there is seldom a single notion within the university about the role of higher education, in Botswana there was a very strong emphasis in both the interviews and the key planning and strategy documents that the university must be connected, through its role as 'the knowledge institution', to national development. The knowledge economy notion ran concurrent with that of the instrument for development notion but, interestingly, the latter was directed at government and business, while there was very little mention of linkages to communities, particularly in the strategic plans.

The discourse was certainly moving away from a more traditional 'ancillary' view where the main task is to train civil service and professionals. The two more established discourses were between an autonomous institution training relevant person power and the need to be more involved in community service. The engine notion was clearly growing, particularly amongst leadership, but it was not quite prevalent.

TABLE 11 **Comparing national and institutional notions of the role of higher education in Botswana**

Notions	National stakeholders		University stakeholders	
Ancillary	•	Officially not, but frequently articulated	•	University key for development
Self-governing	☐	Ambiguous towards autonomy	☐	Present amongst some senior academics, but not leadership
Instrument for development agendas	■	Feel university is not doing enough	☐	Strong service orientation amongst some staff
Engine for development	☐	Mainly in new education policy	☐	Increasing orientation towards its importance

Key:

■ Strong   ☐ Present   • Absent

FINDINGS

- In terms of notions of the role of the university in development, at the national level there was quite a strong leaning towards the instrument for development approach, while at the university there were a number of competing notions but a stronger inclination towards the notion of the university as ancillary.
- At neither national nor institutional levels was there agreement about the role of the university in development. It was quite surprising that amongst university leadership there was not a stronger engine of development approach, particularly in the context of the institution's involvement in the innovation hubs.

5.3   The academic core of the University of Botswana

The analysis of the university's academic core presented in the case study report was undertaken on the basis of the rating of seven key indicators as 'strong', 'medium' or 'weak'. The data on which the ratings are based are contained in the detailed case study report.[16] The seven indicators and their ratings are presented in Table 12.

TABLE 12 University of Botswana: Rating of the academic core

	Indicator	Rating (strong/medium/weak)*
1	Science, engineering and technology enrolments and graduations	SET enrolments = 22% for both 2001 and 2007
2	Postgraduate/undergraduate enrolments ratio Masters/PhD enrolment ratio	Postgraduates = 9% of enrolments (2007); Doctorates = 5% of combined masters/doctoral total (2007)
3	Teaching load: Academic staff–student ratio	FTE student: academic ratio = 17:1 (2007)
4	Proportion of academic staff with doctorates	31% of academics with doctorates (2007)
5	Research income per permanent academic staff member**	Very low at PPP$ 2 000
6	Doctoral graduates	Graduates in 2007 constituted 0.66% of permanent academics
7	Research publications	Research productivity poor (0.16 per academic). Ratios of outputs to academic staff well below research university targets

Key:

■ Strong   ▨ Medium   ☐ Weak

* Refer to Appendix F for a detailed descriptions of the academic core rating categories.

** No specific information provided on research funding. Research income assumed to be 1% of total income.

---

16   The Botswana and University of Botswana case study report is available at www.chet.org.za.

The following observations can be made about the academic core data for the University of Botswana:

1. **SET enrolments**: The university's SET enrolments grew from 2 600 in 2001 to 3 600 in 2007. The average annual SET growth rate was 5.6% over this period, which was the same rate as that for total enrolments. The proportion of SET students remained low at 22% in 2007. The university's SET graduation rate dropped over the period.

2. **Postgraduate enrolments**: The university's proportion of postgraduate students in its total enrolment remained low. This proportion was only 7% in 2001 and 9% in 2007. The university did, however, report a rapid growth in masters enrolments, which increased from 493 in 2001 to 951 in 2007. The masters graduates total did not, however, increase at the same rate as the enrolment total, which implies that the institution might have begun to experience some problems with masters graduation rates. Doctoral enrolments remained low over the period, reaching a total of 41 in 2007 which was 0.3% of the university's total student enrolment in 2007.

3. **Teaching load**: Between 2001 and 2007, the university's full-time equivalent (FTE) academic staff total grew at half the average annual growth rate in FTE students. As a consequence, its FTE student to FTE academic staff ratio increased from 14:1 in 2001 to 17:1 in 2007. Its 2007 ratio could nevertheless be regarded as a satisfactory one for a university which had only 22% of its students in SET programmes. The university's permanent academics must, in 2007, have had reasonable teaching loads, even though the university appeared to employ no temporary or part-time academic staff.

4. **Qualifications of staff**: In 2007, 31% of the university's permanent academic staff had doctorates as their highest formal qualifications.

5. **Research funding**: The estimates calculated suggest that the university would not be able to fund its research activities adequately.

6. **Doctoral graduates**: Doctoral graduates increased from three in 2001 to four in 2007, which was, along with Eduardo Mondlane University, the lowest in the sample. The very low ratio of 0.66% of doctoral graduates to permanent academic staff means that the university would have difficulty reproducing itself.

7. **Research publications**: In terms of research publications, the university's output was low. Its 2007 ratio of publication units per permanent academic was, at 0.16, well below the ratio of 0.50 which had been set as a target for South Africa's research universities.

In terms of input variables, the university had teaching loads which should enable its academic staff to support research activities. However, the problem seems to be in the low percentage of staff with doctorates, low postgraduate enrolments and very low research income (the university, not the government, was making strenuous efforts to increase research income). On the output side, the SET graduation rate was strong, but knowledge production, doctoral graduates and research publications were weak.

The factors that appeared to be weakening the academic core included an incentive system that did not reward knowledge production, a low percentage of staff with doctorates, and low research income. The University of Botswana was clearly facing an enormous challenge to move from the traditional undergraduate teaching university to an institution that could make a more significant contribution to knowledge production and to development.

FINDINGS

- The knowledge production output variables of the academic core did not seem strong enough to enable the university to make a sustainable contribution to development.
- The university was not significantly changing from a predominantly undergraduate teaching institution.
- On the input side, the university scored strong on staff teaching load, and medium on staff qualifications and postgraduate enrolments.
- The university was strong on SET graduation rates, but weak on doctoral graduates and research output.
- The most serious challenges to strengthening the academic core seemed to be to increase research funding, doctoral graduation rates and research outputs.

5.4   Coordination and connectedness

Knowledge policy coordination and implementation in Botswana

Table 13 presents the ratings for the coordination of knowledge policies at the national level. Despite the acceptance of a 'knowledge economy' policy by the Department of Education and parliament, there was still weak, or unsystematic linking of education and economic policies, a weak Ministry of Education (apparently to be strengthened by the Tertiary Education Council) resulting in weak implementation (policies, resources and incentives). Funding for higher education was not strongly supplemented by third-stream income and therefore there was some funding unpredictability. There also seemed to be weak coordination and consensus-building, a lack of formal structures to facilitate coordination, and networks were political rather than promoting productive cooperation.

The establishment of the Human Resource Development Council through the merger of three public sector institutions was, apart from fiscal pressures, an attempt at improved planning, policy co-ordination, oversight and service delivery in term of human resources.

TABLE 13 National coordination of knowledge policies

National rating = 3/9			
Economic development and higher education planning are linked	3 Systematic Formal structures Headed by senior minister	2 Sporadic Clusters/forums	**1 Weak** Occasional meetings
Link between universities and national authorities	3 Specific coordination structures or agencies	2 Some formal structures but no meaningful coordination	1 No structures, and political rather than professional networks
Coordination and consensus building of government agencies involved in higher education	3 Higher education mainstreamed across government departments	2 Intermittent interaction with ineffective forums	1 Higher education issues limited mainly to one ministry or directorate

FINDINGS

- At the national level, there seemed to be many informal interactions, but few institutionalised processes of coordination.
- While there were considerable personal networks between government officials and particular University of Botswana leaders, it was not clear whether this contributed towards strengthening the institution or the sector.

Table 14 summarises the ratings of the indicators relating to the implementation of knowledge policies and activities at both the national and university levels.

TABLE 14 Implementation of knowledge policies and activities in Botswana

National rating = 8/12			
Role of the ministry responsible for higher education	3 Organised ministry with capacity to make predictable allocations	**2** Spots of capacity with some steering instruments	1 Weak capacity with unpredictable allocations
Implementation to 'steer' higher education towards development	3 Strong Instruments such as funding/ special projects that incentivise institutions/individuals	**2 Weak** Occasional grants for special projects	1 Absent No particular incentive funding
Balance/ratio of sources of income for institutions	3 Government, fees and third stream	**2** Mainly government plus student fees	1 Mainly government with external funders
Funding consistency	3 A stable, transparent public funding mechanism based on criteria agreed upon by all actors involved	**2** Funding allocations somewhat predictable but do not allow for long-term planning nor reward enterprising behaviour	1 No clear funding or incentives from government

>>

TABLE 14 Continued

University rating = 10/18			
Specific units, funding or appointments linked to economic development	3 Specific units, funding or appointments	2 Economic development initiatives aspect of a unit or appointment	**1** Mainly ad hoc, staff-initiated operations
Incentives and rewards for development-related activities	3 Incentives/counts towards promotion	**2** Some signals but largely rhetoric	1 No mention
Teaching programmes linked to the labour market	**3** Targets for enrolments in fields considered to be of high economic relevance	2 Some programmes in response to specific industry requests	1 No new programmes linked to labour market
Special programmes linking students to economic development	3 Entrepreneurship, work-based learning and/or incubators for students mainstreamed	2 Ad hoc programmes	**1** No special programmes
Research activities becoming more economy-oriented	3 Research policy/strategy has an economic development focus	**2** Some research agendas have an economic development focus	1 Ad hoc project funding
Levels of government and institutional funding for research	3 High	2 Medium	**1** Low

FINDINGS

- At the national level, one of the weaknesses was implementation, with a continued disagreement about the role of Department of Education and the Tertiary Education Council.
- While the university did have development-related structures and special programmes linking it to development initiatives, the problem was that in too many cases these initiatives were driven by individuals rather than being institutionalised. In addition, these special implementation efforts need to be more connected.
- The university, within tight budget constraints, was trying to strengthen research related to development activities. However, research related to development was not significantly rewarded through incentives beyond the traditional academic promotion system.

The University of Botswana's connectedness to external stakeholders and the academic core

The university had a new engagement strategy that had clear intentions of connecting to government, communities and industry. Amongst others, it intended to establish a facilitating environment for the commercialisation of research and development; to improve opportunities for better employment; and to contribute to sustainable communities where people benefit from improved cultural offerings. Specific strategies included the following:

- Increasing knowledge and technology transfer (including consultancy, contract research, lease of specialist equipment and facilities);
- Increasing student work placements and labour market relevance;
- Participation in the Botswana Innovation Hub;
- Establishment of the Centre for Entrepreneurial Development, and a University Enterprise Unit which would provide support to the development of commerce and industry, technology and development to generate third-stream income; and
- Expansion of health programmes and research.

While the university did appear to have a history of interaction with the government, a number of respondents expressed a somewhat pessimistic view of the relationship. Examples of this included a lack of communication and cooperation between the two; a negative perception of the university on the part of government; and government preferring to use external consultants rather than university expertise. There was very little mention of linkages with industry although there were some developments on the horizon, such as the Botswana Innovation Hub which, if operationalised, would serve to strengthen these linkages. At the same time, there were no real incentives for academics to get involved in engagement or development-related work – whether with government or industry. There was also no specific unit for coordinating internal and external interests.

With regard to the connectedness of development-related activities to the academic core, the articulation and academic ratings applied to the four projects/centres are presented in Figure 4.

FIGURE 4 **Plotting the development-related projects/centres at the University of Botswana**

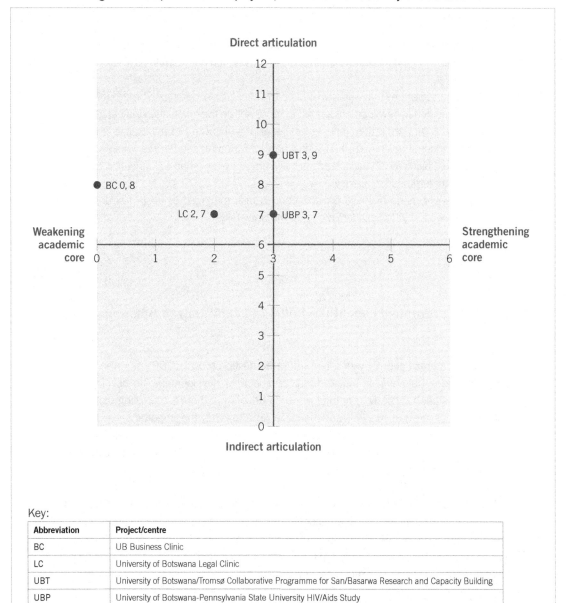

Key:

Abbreviation	Project/centre
BC	UB Business Clinic
LC	University of Botswana Legal Clinic
UBT	University of Botswana/Tromsø Collaborative Programme for San/Basarwa Research and Capacity Building
UBP	University of Botswana-Pennsylvania State University HIV/Aids Study

FINDINGS

- The university was attempting to connect to development through, amongst others, the proposed innovation hubs, but these did not seem to have taken off yet.
- Projects/centres that were considered by university leadership to be strongly connected to development tended to score well on the articulation indicators – in other words, they reflected national priorities (and to a lesser extent institutional objectives), had more than one funding source and, in some cases, plans for financial sustainability, and may have had a connection to an implementation agency.
- However, none of these projects/centres also managed to keep a strong connection to the academic core of the university.

5.5   Concluding comments about the Botswana/University of Botswana case study

Botswana is a small country with a high gross domestic product (GDP), but also a high inequality index, meaning a 'trickle-down' approach to development. Its development approach has been excessively natural resource-driven, but there is a growing realisation that 'diamonds are not forever', and hence a shift towards the importance of human capital. There is access to schooling but participation in higher education is relatively low by international standards (although high within the Southern African region), but is growing. State funding is relatively high but it only reaches the elite.

At the national level, the acceptance by government of the recommendations put forward by the Tertiary Education Council to recognise the importance of human resources, rather than natural resources, as a future driver of development is a very important step. However, as can be seen from the above ratings, this was not reflected in other policies, nor was higher education necessarily seen as a key contributor.

The commitment to knowledge as a basis for development was moderate with a growing awareness, but not with a significant shift in resources yet. Botswana's higher education system's ability to respond to the needs of the knowledge economy could be characterised as 'poor', as is the capacity/potential for research and innovation. However, there was a growing emphasis on moving towards a knowledge economy and a high-skills approach, with a new science and technology university and the planned innovation hubs. But the country had not yet invested sufficiently in either the universities or innovation, nor had it provided appropriate incentives for partnerships.

At the time of the study, there was not yet effective linking of education and economic planning, nor acceptance of the knowledge economy approach across departments. Coordination structures were weak or unsystematic and networks were more political than 'productive'.

What were some of the factors impacting on the University of Botswana's capacity to contribute to development?

In terms of input variables, the university had a favourable staff teaching load, and an acceptable proportion of staff with doctorates. In terms of output variables, such as the production of research publications and of doctoral graduates, the university performed poorly in comparison to South Africa's research-intensive universities. The key factors that seemed to be weakening the academic core were (a) the low proportion of postgraduate students, (b) the low numbers of students in the doctoral research stream, and (c) the poor output of research publications. A positive development was that the university had not experienced a rapid growth in student enrolments, which should enable it to consolidate its programme offerings, and move to increase enrolments in SET.

In terms of articulation, it seemed that from the side of government there was not enough support, either financially or in terms of interaction, to help the university to move from a more traditional undergraduate teaching institution to strengthening postgraduate programmes and producing new knowledge. The engagement strategy and the innovation hubs are certainly moves in the right direction, but these need more implementation support.

As was reflected in the academic core summary above, within the institution the new vision of becoming an increased skills-, research- and innovation-orientated partner and driver in a new development path had not been realised. Both government and the university were having problems in making tough reallocation decisions, meaning that the pact was not strong enough to make unpopular trade-offs, resulting in few real resource redistributions to implement the new vision.

6

Ghana and the University of Ghana

6.1   The higher education and economic development context in Ghana

How did Ghana fare in meeting the 'preconditions' for an effective and productive relationship between higher education and economic development identified by Pillay's (2010b) investigation of three successful systems?

High-quality schooling: In the sub-Saharan African context, participation rates are relatively high at both the primary and secondary levels. In Ghana, the gross enrolment ratio in primary education was 98% in 2006 and the net enrolment ratio was 72%. However, this still left the country far short of achieving universal primary education. The secondary schooling participation rates are encouraging and substantially higher than the sub-Saharan African averages. In 2006, the gross enrolment ratio in secondary schooling was 49% and the net enrolment ratio was 45% (UNESCO 2009). The corresponding averages for sub-Saharan Africa were 32% and 25%. The Ghanaian figures were close to developing country averages (60% and 53%, respectively). Moreover, there is some evidence that the schooling system was relatively efficient and of reasonably good quality. For example, the survival rate to the last grade of primary schooling was 76% in 2006 (the average for sub-Saharan Africa was 67%, and that for developing countries 81%) (ibid.). Furthermore, the Global Innovation Index ranks Ghana relatively high on some education indicators such as 'quality of educational institutions' (ranked 68 compared to its overall GII ranking of 108) and 'quality of the educational system' (it is ranked at 73) (INSEAD 2010). All of this suggests that while access and equity remain pressing challenges in the schooling system, Ghana does have a small and growing base of good quality schooling on which to build a better quality higher education system.

Effective economic and education planning: An important institutional mechanism has been created for planning, namely the National Development Planning Commission. However, there was little evidence of linking economic and education planning. At best there was some degree of commitment to a cross-cutting issue such as human resources development, which includes education, as well as a recognition of the importance of education for economic growth.

The role of the state: The state was playing an important role with respect to funding, as well as encouraging private sector provision of higher education. However, the state's policy documents did not clearly articulate the role of higher education in economic development, or its role in contributing to the knowledge economy.

Partnerships: In general, there was no evidence of partnerships between the state, the universities and the private sector.

Institutional differentiation: There was evidence of significant differentiation amongst universities (e.g. University of Ghana vs. Kwame Nkrumah University of Technology) and across the system (universities vs. polytechnics).

Quality: There was some evidence that the quality of schooling is relatively good although the WEF's Global Competitiveness Index suggests otherwise.

Funding: State funding of tertiary education was relatively high. The state had also encouraged diversified funding of both students (through the student loan fund) and institutions (through encouraging internally-generated funds).

Innovation: At the time of the study, Ghana had not invested sufficiently either in its universities or in its private sector, nor had it provided appropriate incentives for partnerships to develop between these groups.

6.2   Evidence of a pact around the role of higher education in Ghana?

Ghana's indicator ratings for the role of knowledge and universities in national and institutional policies and plans are presented in Table 15.

At the national level, the orientation seemed to be more on a traditional approach to producing human resources for the economy and poverty alleviation. The knowledge economy and research and innovation were only mentioned occasionally. This absence was reflected in national policy, resource reallocation and a lack of incentives.

At the institutional level, the narrative at the university was surprisingly traditional – 'teaching, research and extension services'. While this was presented as an orientation towards development ("to make a more relevant and tangible contribution to the improvement of the standards of living of the nation"), as can be seen from the ratings, there was not a knowledge economy discourse, nor was this development orientation reflected in policies, structures or incentives. The concern expressed about academic priorities (core) was still cast in the undifferentiated teaching-research-service discourse.

TABLE 15 **Role for knowledge and universities in development in Ghana**

National rating = 3/6			
The concept of a knowledge economy features in the national development plan	3 Strong Appears in a number of policies	2 Weak Only mentioned in one policy	**1 Absent** Not mentioned at all
A role for higher education in development in national policies and plans	3 Prevalent Clearly mentioned in development policies	**2 Weak**	1 Absent
University rating = 2/6			
Concept of a knowledge economy features in institutional policies and plans	3 Features strongly in strategic plan and/or research policy/ strategy	2 Vague reference in strategic plan or research policy	**1** Not mentioned at all
Institutional policies with regard to the university's role in economic development	3 Institutional policy	2 Embedded in strategic plan, research policy, etc.	**1** No formal policies

FINDINGS

- At both national and institutional levels there was only sporadic mention of the knowledge economy, and no agreement (pact) about a development model and the role of higher education in development.
- There was no broad agreement that knowledge, and by implication higher education, is key to development.

Notions of the role of knowledge and universities in development

Table 16 summarises the notions of the role of higher education held by national and institutional stakeholders, and indicates whether the notion was strong, prevalent, present or absent altogether.

It appeared that during the period of study (2009/early 2010), there was still a residue of the traditional ancillary notion, namely that higher education must produce person power. In addition, although it was agreed that the university is an institution that is important in national development, in producing high-level bureaucrats, and in producing scientific knowledge, the notion that there is no need for a direct role in national development was present. While there was certainly a growing awareness of the production of new knowledge and high-end skills as a driver for development, it was not yet being operationalised in a range of government and institutional policies.

TABLE 16 Comparing national and institutional notions of the role of higher education in Ghana

Notions	National stakeholders		University stakeholders	
Ancillary	■	Ambiguous about the role of higher in development	□	Still present, despite new awareness of the need for a development orientation
Self-governing	□	Strong expectation to produce human capital	■	Very much present in the teaching-research-service orientation
Instrument for development agendas	○	Government wants to make more use of university expertise	○	Consultancy mainly for donors and government
Engine for development	□	Not much awareness	○	Surprisingly absent in university discourse and policies

Key:

■ Strong   □ Present   ○ Absent

FINDINGS

- In terms of notions of the role of the university in development, at the national level there was considerable ambiguity about the role of the university while at the institutional level there was a strong leaning towards self-governance.
- At neither national nor institutional levels was there agreement about the role of the university in development. It was quite surprising that amongst university leadership there was such low support for a knowledge economy approach.

6.3   The academic core of the University of Ghana

The analysis of the university's academic core presented in the case study report was undertaken on the basis of the rating of seven key indicators as 'strong', 'medium' or 'weak'. The data on which the ratings are based are contained in the detailed case study report.[17] The seven indicators and their ratings are presented in Table 17.

---

17   The Ghana and University of Ghana case study report is available at www.chet.org.za.

TABLE 17 **University of Ghana: Rating of the academic core**

	Indicator	Rating (strong/medium/weak)*
1	Science, engineering and technology enrolments and graduations	SET students = 17% in 2007. Only 60% of SET intakes expected to graduate
2	Postgraduate/undergraduate enrolments ratio Masters/PhD enrolment ratio	Proportion of postgraduates fell from 12% in 2001 to 6% in 2007. Ratio of masters to doctoral enrolments high at 16:1
3	Teaching load: Academic staff–student ratio	Overall ratio 26:1 in 2007, and particularly favourable in SET
4	Proportion of academic staff with doctorates	47% of permanent academics have doctorates, but a high proportion of 42% have only masters
5	Research income per permanent academic staff member**	Low at PPP$ 3 4000
6	Doctoral graduates	Graduates in 2007 constituted 0.17% of permanent academics
7	Research publications	Outputs in 2007 is 0.13 of publications per permanent academic

Key:

▪ Strong   ▫ Medium   ☐ Weak

* Refer to Appendix F for a detailed descriptions of the academic core rating categories.

** No specific information provided on research funding. Research income assumed to be 3% of total income.

The following observations can be made about the academic core data for the University of Ghana:

1. **SET enrolments**: The university's SET enrolments grew from 3 200 in 2001 to 4 500 in 2007, at an average annual rate of 5.8%. Because the average annual growth rate for all programmes was 10.8% over this period, the proportion of SET students dropped from 22% in 2001 to only 17% in 2007. The university's SET graduation rate, despite the slow growth in enrolments, fell over the period. Only about 60% of students entering SET programmes can be expected to complete their qualifications.

2. **Postgraduate enrolments**: The university's proportion of postgraduate students in its total enrolment fell from 12% in 2001 to 6% in 2007. This resulted from a rapid increase in undergraduate enrolments, during a period in which postgraduate enrolments increased at an average annual rate of less than 1%. Masters enrolments grew from 1 344 in 2001 to 1 580 in 2007, an average annual increase of 2.7%. The masters graduates total increased at only half the rate of the enrolment total, but the masters graduation rate remained satisfactory. Doctoral enrolments increased from 69 in 2001 to 102 in 2007, but still had a share of only 6% of the masters plus doctors total. This implies that the flow of masters graduates into doctoral studies may not have been high enough to sustain strong research activities. Doctoral graduation rates remained low over the period.

3. **Teaching load**: Between 2001 and 2007, the university's FTE academic staff total grew at about one third of the annual growth rate in FTE students. Its average FTE student to FTE academic staff ratio, as a consequence, rose from 16:1 in 2001 to 26:1 in 2007. Its SET ratio and its humanities plus education ratios remained favourable by South African standards. Its business/management ratio, as is the case with many other universities, was an unacceptably high 47:1 in 2007. A conclusion which can be drawn is that the university's permanent academics in the fields of SET and humanities must, in 2007, have had teaching loads at levels which would make it difficult for academics to engage in research activities, including the supervision of research students.

4. **Qualifications of staff**: In 2007, 47% of the university's permanent academic staff had doctorates as their highest formal qualifications. It is worth noting that, in 2007, 330 permanent academics (42% of the total) had masters degrees as their highest formal qualification. These academics could be brought into doctoral programmes and could, in this way, support the university's research activities.

5. **Research funding**: The estimates calculated suggest that the university research funding might not be sufficient to sustain strong research activities.

6. **Doctoral graduates**: Doctoral graduates increased from 9 in 2001 to 11 in 2007, which is an amazing 46%, but from a very low base. A very positive development was that the doctoral enrolments also doubled over the same period. However, the very low ratio of 0.17% of doctoral graduates to permanent academic staff means that the university would have difficulty reproducing itself.

7. **Research publications**: In terms of research publications, the university's output was low. Its 2007 ratio of publication units per permanent academic was, at 0.13, well below the ratio of 0.50 which has been set as a target for South Africa's research universities.

In terms of input variables, the university had teaching loads which should enable its academic staff to support research activities. It also had a satisfactory proportion of academic staff with doctorates, and a pool of staff with masters degrees who should be encouraged to join research programmes as doctoral students. In terms of output variables, such as the production of research publications and of doctoral graduates, the university's performance was poor. The key factors that seemed to be weakening the academic core were (a) the low and declining proportion of SET students; (b) the rapid increase in humanities plus education enrolments; (c) the low proportions of masters and doctoral students; (d) the low output of doctoral graduates; (e) a shortage of research funding; and (f) the poor output of research publications. A positive development is that the university was experiencing a growth in masters enrolments and was sustaining masters graduation rates. Staff and others who have obtained masters degrees could prove to be important for improving research output.

FINDINGS

- The knowledge production output variables of the academic core did not seem strong enough to enable the university to make a sustained contribution to development.
- The university was not significantly changing from a predominantly undergraduate teaching institution.
- On the input side, the university scores medium on staff teaching load, staff qualifications and postgraduate enrolments.
- The university scored weak on all three output variables: SET graduation rate, doctoral graduates and research output.
- The most serious challenges to strengthening the academic core seemed to be to increase research funding, doctoral graduation rates and research outputs.

6.4   Coordination and connectedness

Knowledge policy coordination and implementation in Ghana

Table 18 presents the ratings for the coordination of knowledge policies at the national level. There were very few formal linkages and coordination between different departments and different policies. Significant progress had been made in terms of developing the appropriate institutional mechanisms (e.g. the National Council for Tertiary Education in the education sector, and the National Development Planning Commission in the Ministry of Finance and Economic Planning). However, little effort had been put into coordinating the implementation of cross-cutting issues such as higher education and development. While there were many informal linkages between individual academics and units and particular ministries, there were no formal structures linking the university to government.

TABLE 18 National coordination of knowledge policies in Ghana

National rating = 3/9			
Economic development and higher education planning are linked	3 Systematic Formal structures Headed by senior minister	2 Sporadic Clusters/forums	**1 Weak** Occasional meetings
Link between universities and national authorities	3 Specific coordination structures or agencies	2 Some formal structures but no meaningful coordination	1 No structures, and political rather than professional networks
Coordination and consensus building of government agencies involved in higher education	3 Higher education mainstreamed across government departments	2 Intermittent interaction with ineffective forums	1 Higher education issues limited mainly to one ministry or directorate

FINDINGS

- At the national level, there seemed to be many informal interactions, but few institutionalised processes.
- While there were considerable personal networks between government officials and particular university leaders, it was not clear whether this contributed towards strengthening the institution or the sector.

Table 19 summarises the ratings of the indicators relating to the implementation of knowledge policies and activities at both the national and university levels.

TABLE 19 Implementation of knowledge policies and activities in Ghana

National rating = 8/12			
Role of the ministry responsible for higher education	3 Organised ministry with capacity to make predictable allocations	**2** Spots of capacity with some steering instruments	1 Weak capacity with unpredictable allocations
Implementation to 'steer' higher education towards development	3 Strong Instruments such as funding/ special projects that incentivise institutions/individuals	2 Weak Occasional grants for special projects	**1 Absent** No particular incentive funding
Balance/ratio of sources of income for institutions	**3** Government, fees and third stream	2 Mainly government plus student fees	1 Mainly government with external funders
Funding consistency	3 A stable, transparent public funding mechanism based on criteria agreed upon by all actors involved	**2** Funding allocations somewhat predictable but do not allow for long-term planning nor reward enterprising behaviour	1 No clear funding or incentives from government
University rating = 8/18			
Specific units, funding or appointments linked to economic development	3 Specific units, funding or appointments	2 Economic development initiatives aspect of a unit or appointment	**1** Mainly ad hoc, staff-initiated operations
Incentives and rewards for development-related activities	3 Incentives/counts towards promotion	2 Some signals but largely rhetoric	**1** No mention
Teaching programmes linked to the labour market	3 Targets for enrolments in fields considered to be of high economic relevance	**2** Some programmes in response to specific industry requests	1 No new programmes linked to labour market
Special programmes linking students to economic development	3 Entrepreneurship, work-based learning and/or incubators for students mainstreamed	2 Ad hoc programmes	**1** No special programmes
Research activities are becoming more economy-oriented	3 Research policy/strategy has an economic development focus	**2** Some research agendas have an economic development focus	1 Ad hoc project funding
Levels of government and institutional funding for research	3 High	2 Medium	**1** Low

FINDINGS

- At the national level, one of the weaknesses was implementation, but with a stronger emerging role for the National Council for Tertiary Education.
- While the university did have development-related structures and special programmes linking it to development initiatives, the problem was that in too many cases these initiatives were driven by individuals rather than being institutionalised. In addition, these special implementation efforts need to be more connected.
- The university, within tight budget constraints, was trying to increase research related to development activities, but research related to development was not significantly rewarded through incentives beyond the traditional academic promotion system.

The University of Ghana's connectedness to external stakeholders and the academic core

There was very little coordination of government and donor agendas by the university. The most common practice was for contracts to be signed directly between the external source of funds and the individual researcher. It was also mentioned that it was very difficult to raise funds to deal with health issues that are of national concern when these were not on foreign donor agendas. Also mentioned was the tension between donor and country priorities, as well as traditional forms of academic assessment.

Linkages between the university and government and industry seemed to be more at the level of individual academics and units and not at an institutional level. And, instead of any formal, structured engagement between university and government, interactions appeared to be very informal and ad hoc.

With regard to the connectedness of development-related activities to the academic core, the articulation and academic ratings applied to the six projects/centres are presented in Figure 5.

FIGURE 5 **Plotting the development-related projects/centres at the University of Ghana**

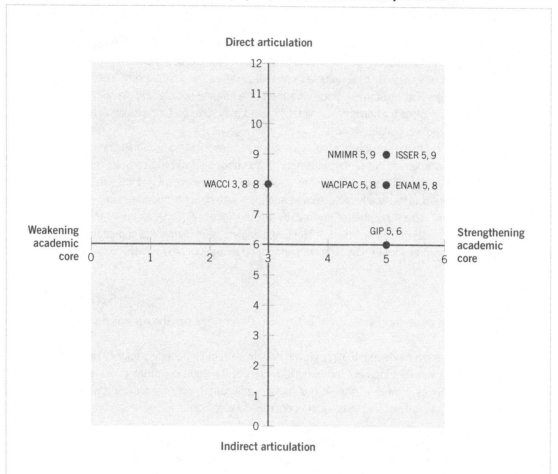

Key:

Abbreviation	Project/centre
GIP	Gates Institute Partnership Project for Population, Family and Reproductive Health
NMIMR	Noguchi Memorial Institute for Medical Research
WACCI	West Africa Centre for Crop Improvement
WACIPAC	West African Centre for International Parasite Control
ENAM	Enhancing Child Nutrition Through Animal Source Food Management
ISSER	Institute of Statistical Social and Economic Research

FINDINGS

- Projects/centres that were considered by university leadership to be strongly connected to development tended to score well on the articulation indicators – in other words, they reflected national priorities (and to a lesser extent institutional objectives), had more than one funding source and, in some cases, plans for financial sustainability, and may have had a connection to an implementation agency.
- Most of these projects/centres also managed to keep a strong connection to the academic core of the university. Of the universities in the sample, the University of Ghana scored the strongest on development projects that connect to the academic core and articulate with national priorities.
- There were a number of 'exemplary' development projects/centres at the University of Ghana. The problem is scale: there were simply not enough of these, and some seem overly dependent on exceptional individuals.

6.5 Concluding comments about the Ghana/University of Ghana case study

Ghana has been a moderate- to high-growth country with the lowest discrepancy between GDP and Human Development Index (HDI) ratings of the eight countries in our sample (see Appendix A). However, while it has had a significant impact on reducing absolute poverty, this has not resulted in broader economic development.

The higher education landscape is differentiating, and participation rates growing, particularly in the African context. In both government and the university the orientation seemed to be more on a traditional approach to producing human resources for the economy and poverty alleviation. The knowledge economy and research and innovation were only mentioned occasionally. A positive was the new National Science, Technology and Innovation Policy which states that Ghana's ambition was to become a middle-income country. This would require a vision of development which fully applies and integrates science, technology and innovation into national development strategies to harness fully the nation's total science and technology capacity to achieve national objectives for poverty reduction, competitiveness of enterprises, sustainable environmental management and industrial growth.

However, this intention was not present across policies, or in resource reallocation. Furthermore, a change of incentives, and the linkages and coordination which were developing, were not yet formalised. Within the university, the narrative about the role of the university was surprisingly traditional, focussing on teaching, research and extension services. There was neither a strong knowledge economy discourse, nor was this development orientation reflected in policies, structures or incentives.

In conclusion, in neither government nor the university did it seem that there was a strong agreement on the role of the university in development.

7

Kenya and the University of Nairobi

7.1 The higher education and economic development context in Kenya

How did Kenya fare in meeting the 'preconditions' for an effective and productive relationship between higher education and economic development identified by Pillay's (2010b) investigation of three successful systems?

High-quality schooling: Participation rates were relatively low at both the primary and secondary levels. The net enrolment ratio in primary education increased significantly from 63% in 1999 to 75% in 2006, but still left the country far short of achieving universal primary education. The secondary schooling participation rates compared favourably with most African countries. In 2006, the gross enrolment ratio in secondary schooling was 50% and the net enrolment ratio was 42% (UNESCO 2009). The corresponding averages for sub-Saharan Africa were 32% and 25%, and for developing countries 60% and 53%, respectively. Both the Global Competitiveness and Global Innovation Index reports comment favourably on the quality of Kenyan schooling. The survival rate to the last grade of primary schooling was 84% in 2006 (the average for sub-Saharan Africa was 67%, and that for developing countries 81%) Moreover, the average rate of repetition in primary schooling was a low 6% (ibid.).

Effective economic and education planning: There was acknowledgment of the link between education and economic development but little effort had been made to put in place the appropriate policies and necessary institutional mechanisms in government to effect a closer coordination of education and economic policies.

The role of the state: The state was playing an important role with respect to funding, as well as encouraging private sector provision of higher education. The state's policy documents gave prominence to the role of tertiary education in development and to the role of science and technology as well.

Partnerships: In general, no evidence could be gleaned of partnerships between the state, the universities and the private sector.

Institutional differentiation: Substantial differentiation occurred in the higher education system with the presence of universities, university colleges, polytechnics, teacher training colleges and other colleges. Within the university sector, less differentiation occurred with all institutions aspiring to becoming teaching and research institutions, with significant duplication of high-cost faculties such as medicine.

Quality: Pockets of good to high quality existed in the higher education sector, especially with respect to the University of Nairobi. However, quality needs to become a much more widespread feature of the higher education system.

Funding: State funding of tertiary education was low in absolute terms given the extent of need and the imperative to increase access and enhance equity.

Innovation: Kenya was ranked relatively high in the Global Innovation Index, especially in terms of its 'innovation inputs'. It therefore had the basic ingredients for innovation and participation in the knowledge economy but appeared to be incapable, at the time of the study, of translating this into appropriate inputs. However, there were two encouraging features with respect to innovation and prospects for the knowledge economy. The first was the merging of higher education and science and technology into one ministry. The second was the policy proposals that had been developed to define the role of science and technology in economic development.

7.2 Evidence of a pact around the role of higher education in Kenya?

Kenya's indicator ratings for the role of knowledge and universities in national and institutional policies and plans are presented in Table 20.

At the national level, Kenya was certainly moving in the direction of a knowledge-driven economy through important initiatives such as *Kenya Vision 2030,* as well as the establishment of a Ministry of Higher Education, Science and Technology – a move which recognises the critical role played by R&D in accelerating economic development in newly-industrialising countries. *Vision 2030* also argues for creating globally competitive and adaptive human resources based on quality education, training and research. However, there was limited evidence that this vision was broadly accepted and, as was pointed out by a respondent, there was no specific role outlined for universities. Also, the ministry responsible for higher education had only spots of capacity to steer the system, funding allocation was only somewhat predictable, and there were no particular incentives to steer the system in the direction of the new vision. One strength was a differentiated system with multiple sources of funding. Despite the fact that policy coordination was in the President's Office – an approach tried and failed in South Africa – coordination of policy across departments, and between government and universities, was at most intermittent.

At the University of Nairobi, reference was made in the strategic plan to the knowledge economy and to the university's role in economic development, but these references were weaker than in the previous strategic plan. The strategic plan referred to teaching and learning as the core business of the university, while innovation and R&D were described as issues the university must address. Despite a number of senior institutional leaders saying in different ways that research is the principal activity that distinguishes the university from other tertiary institutions, both government and institutional support for research was, in the words of a number of respondents, negligible. Furthermore, neither the National Council for Science and Technology nor the Commission for Higher Education had, at the time of the study, played much of a role in raising significant research funding. Rather surprising is that despite the policy commitment to high-level skills training and labour market relevance, programmes linking academics and students to the labour market were mostly ad hoc and not institutionalised.

TABLE 20 **Role for knowledge and universities in development in Kenya**

National rating = 6/6			
The concept of a knowledge economy features in the national development plan	**3 Strong** Appears in a number of policies	2 Weak Only mentioned in one policy	1 Absent Not mentioned at all
A role for higher education in development in national policies and plans	**3 Prevalent** Clearly mentioned in development policies	2 Weak	1 Absent
University rating = 4/6			
Concept of a knowledge economy features in institutional policies and plans	3 Features strongly in strategic plan and/or research policy/strategy	**2** Vague reference in strategic plan or research policy	1 Not mentioned at all
Institutional policies with regard to the university's role in economic development	3 Institutional policy	**2** Embedded in strategic plan, research policy, etc.	1 No formal policies

FINDINGS

- In certain government departments there was a strong emphasis on the knowledge economy. However, despite *Vision 2030*, there was a lack of clarity and agreement (pact) about a development model and the role of higher education in development.
- There was no broad agreement that knowledge, and by implication higher education, is key to development.
- The reorganisation of the ministry showed an emerging awareness about the importance of the knowledge economy approach, perhaps more so at government than at university level.

Notions of the role of knowledge and universities in development

Table 21 summarises the notions of the role of higher education held by national and institutional stakeholders, and indicates whether the notion was strong, prevalent, present or absent altogether.

While there was widespread support for the notion of higher education contributing to development, there was neither in the national *Vision 2030* nor in the university's strategic plan, a clear vision or notion as to how this was to happen. Interestingly, it seemed that while the government had moved towards more policy emphasis on research and innovation, the university had somewhat moved away from it. The dominant positions seemed to be between making a more direct instrumentalist contribution to community and industry development, and the more traditional self-governance approach, but with the emphasis on teaching and learning, not on R&D. For both government and university, the engine of development model was still largely symbolic policy.

TABLE 21 Comparing national and institutional notions of the role of higher education in Kenya

Notions		National stakeholders		University stakeholders
Ancillary	•	Strong feeling that university must be involved	•	Broadly supportive for contributing to *Vision 2030*
Self-governing	☐	University important for development, but not clear on the role	■	Oscillate between teaching-learning and consultancy and research
Instrument for development agendas	☐	Expectation that university should make a more direct contribution to solving social and health problems	■	Still a strong belief amongst academics
Engine for development	■	Strongly reflected in future vision, but not in reallocation of resources	☐	Strong on rhetoric, but seem to be vacillating

Key:

■ Strong ☐ Present • Absent

FINDINGS

- At the national level there was quite a strong leaning towards the engine of development approach, combined with a more direct instrumental approach, while at the university there was a more traditional divide between instrumental and self-governance.
- At neither the national nor the institutional level was there agreement about the role of the university in development. It is quite surprising that amongst university leadership there was such low support for a knowledge economy approach.

7.3   The academic core of the University of Nairobi

The analysis of the university's academic core presented in the case study report was undertaken on the basis of the rating of seven key indicators as 'strong', 'medium' or 'weak'. The data on which the ratings are based are contained in the detailed case study report.[18] The seven indicators and their ratings are presented in Table 22.

TABLE 22 University of Nairobi: Rating of the academic core

	Indicator	Rating (strong/medium/weak)*
1	Science, engineering and technology enrolments and graduations	SET students = 31% in 2007, but output poor: Only 50% of SET intakes expected to graduate
2	Postgraduate/undergraduate enrolments ratio Masters/PhD enrolment ratio	Proportion of postgraduates fell from 20% in 2001 to 16% in 2007. Ratio of masters to doctoral enrolments very high at 21:1
3	Teaching load: Academic staff–student ratio	Overall ratio 18:1 in 2007, and 9:1 in SET
4	Proportion of academic staff with doctorates	71% of permanent academics have doctorates
5	Research income per permanent academic staff member**	Low at PPP$ 5 300
6	Doctoral graduates	Graduates in 2007 constituted 2.5% of permanent academics
7	Research publications	Outputs in 2007 is 0.11 of publications per permanent academic

Key:

▪ Strong   ▫ Medium   ☐ Weak

* Refer to Appendix F for a detailed descriptions of the academic core rating categories.

** No specific information provided on research funding. Research income assumed to be 3% of total income.

The following observations can be made about the academic core data for the University of Nairobi:

1. **SET enrolments**: The university's SET enrolments grew from 7 600 in 2001 to 12 300 in 2007, at an average annual rate of 8.4%. The proportion of SET students dropped from 33% in 2001 to 31% in 2007. The SET graduation rate, taking account of the full period 2001–2007, was poor. Only 50% of students entering SET programmes could be expected to complete their qualifications.

2. **Postgraduate enrolments**: The proportion of postgraduate students in the university's total enrolment fell from 20% in 2001 to 16% in 2007, mainly because of the rapid growth in undergraduate enrolments. Masters enrolments grew from 3 937 in 2001 to 6 145 in 2007, an average annual increase of 10.4%. However, doctoral enrolments fell from 190 in 2001 to only 62 in 2007. This implies that the university's increased total masters graduates were not moving into doctoral studies.

---

18   The Kenya and University of Nairobi case study report is available at www.chet.org.za.

3. **Teaching load**: Between 2001 and 2007, the university's FTE academic staff total grew at an average annual growth rate of 1%, while FTE students increased at an average annual rate of nearly 8%. Its average FTE student to FTE academic staff ratio, as a consequence, rose from 12:1 in 2001 to 18:1 in 2007. Its SET ratio remained nevertheless remained favourable by South African standards, being only 9:1 in 2007. Its business/management ratio, as is the case with many other universities, was unacceptably high at 42:1 in 2007. A conclusion which can be drawn is that the university's permanent academics in the fields of SET must, in 2007, have had teaching loads at levels which should have enabled them to engage in research activities, including the supervision of research students.

4. **Qualifications of staff**: In 2007, more than 900 (or 71%) of the university's permanent academic staff had doctorates as their highest formal qualifications. This proportion of 71% was well above the highest reported by South African universities.

5. **Research funding**: The estimates calculated suggest that the university's research funding might not be sufficient to sustain strong research activities.

6. **Doctoral graduates**: There was an increase in doctoral graduates of 3.5% between 2001 and 2007, but from a rather low base of 26, which results in the very low ratio of 2.5% of doctoral graduates to permanent academic staff. The doctoral enrolments decreased from 190 in 2001 to 62 in 2007 – a rather dramatic drop which will surely affect future graduate outputs.

7. **Research publications**: In terms of research publications, the university's output was low. Its 2007 ratio of publication units per permanent academic was, at 0.11, well below the ratio of 0.50 which has been set as a target for South Africa's research universities.

In terms of input variables, the university had teaching loads, particularly in SET, which should enable its academic staff to support research activities. It also had a substantial total of more than 900 academic staff with doctorates and fast-growing masters-level enrolments. The university's output performance, despite these advantages in its inputs, was poor. Graduation rates in SET were low. The through-flow from masters to doctorate was very low and the production of doctoral graduates and research articles was also low. The key factors that seemed to be weakening the academic core were (a) the inefficient outputs of SET graduates, (b) the low proportions of postgraduate students, and in particular doctoral students, (c) the low output of doctoral graduates, and (d) the poor output of research publications. A positive development is that the university is experiencing a growth in masters enrolments, and graduates from these programmes could prove to be important inputs for future research programmes. However, this would require that the conditions for through-flow are improved.

The factors that appeared to be weakening the academic core included an incentive system that did not reward knowledge production, and low research income combined with attractive consultancies and additional income-generating teaching opportunities.

FINDINGS

- The knowledge production output variables of the academic core did not seem strong enough to enable the university to make a sustainable contribution to development.
- The university was not significantly changing from a predominantly under-graduate teaching institution, with strength in SET and business studies.
- On the input side, the university scored strong on masters and doctoral enrolments (despite the decline in the latter), staff teaching load and, particularly, staff qualifications (the highest in the sample).
- The university scored weak on all three output variables, despite a strong showing on the input side.
- The most serious challenges to strengthening the academic core seemed to be to increasing research funding, doctoral graduation rates and research outputs.

7.4 Coordination and connectedness

Knowledge policy coordination and implementation in Kenya

Table 23 presents the ratings for the coordination of knowledge policies at the national level.

TABLE 23 National coordination of knowledge policies in Kenya

National rating = 6/9			
Economic development and higher education planning are linked	3 Systematic Formal structures Headed by senior minister	**2 Sporadic** Clusters/forums	1 Weak Occasional meetings
Link between universities and national authorities	3 Specific coordination structures or agencies	**2** Some formal structures but no meaningful coordination	1 No structures, and political rather than professional networks
Coordination and consensus building of government agencies involved in higher education	3 Higher education mainstreamed across government departments	**2** Intermittent interaction with ineffective forums	1 Higher education issues limited mainly to one ministry or directorate

FINDINGS

- At the national level, there were considerable coordination activities, including clusters and the reorganisation of the national ministry.
- While there were personal networks between government officials and particular university leaders, it was not clear whether this contributed towards strengthening the institution or the sector.

Table 24 summarises the ratings of the indicators relating to the implementation of knowledge policies and activities at both the national and university levels. By far the largest proportion of research funding in the University of Nairobi comes from foreign donors. A senior academic commented that in recent years there had been major changes, particularly amongst the American donor agencies such as USAID and Rockefeller, which were no longer funding research in the universities directly, but rather through civil society organisations. According to this respondent, this was leading to fragmentation and projectisation since funding was provided for numerous small, short-term projects rather than for longer-term research programmes.

There was no evidence of specific incentives or rewards to encourage development-related activities. However, the university's previous strategic plan (2005–2010) made reference to the intention to establish rewards (criteria for promotion) for consultancy activities, although it was not clear whether these had been realised. And, while consultancy had been mainstreamed, there did not appear to be any concrete mechanisms in place for incentivising or rewarding development-related activities.

TABLE 24 Implementation of knowledge policies and activities in Kenya

National rating = 8/12		
Role of the ministry responsible for higher education	3 Organised ministry with capacity to make predictable allocations	**2** Spots of capacity with some steering instruments	1 Weak capacity with unpredictable allocations
Implementation to 'steer' higher education towards development	3 Strong Instruments such as funding/ special projects that incentivise institutions/individuals	2 Weak Occasional grants for special projects	**1 Absent** No particular incentive funding
Balance/ratio of sources of income for institutions	**3** Government, fees and third stream	2 Mainly government plus student fees	1 Mainly government with external funders
Funding consistency	3 A stable, transparent public funding mechanism based on criteria agreed upon by all actors involved	**2** Funding allocations somewhat predictable but do not allow for long-term planning nor reward enterprising behaviour	1 No clear funding or incentives from government

TABLE 24 Continued

University rating = 8/18			
Specific units, funding or appointments linked to economic development	3 Specific units, funding or appointments	2 Economic development initiatives aspect of a unit or appointment	**1** Mainly ad hoc, staff-initiated operations
Incentives and rewards for development-related activities	3 Incentives/counts towards promotion	**2** Some signals but largely rhetoric	1 No mention
Teaching programmes linked to the labour market	3 Targets for enrolments in fields considered to be of high economic relevance	2 Some programmes in response to specific industry requests	**1** No new programmes linked to labour market
Special programmes linking students to economic development	3 Entrepreneurship, work-based learning and/or incubators for students mainstreamed	**2** Ad hoc programmes	1 No special programmes
Research activities becoming more economy-oriented	3 Research policy/strategy has an economic development focus	2 Some research agendas have an economic development focus	**1** Ad hoc project funding
Levels of government and institutional funding for research	3 High	2 Medium	**1** Low

FINDINGS

- One of the weaknesses was implementation, both at national and institutional levels.
- While the university did have development-related structures and special programmes linking it to development initiatives, the problem was that in too many cases these initiatives were driven by individuals rather than being institutionalised. In addition, these special implementation efforts need to be more connected.
- Despite policies that extol the importance of research related to development activities, research related to development was not rewarded through incentives beyond the traditional academic promotion system.

The University of Nairobi's connectedness to external stakeholders and the academic core

While there appeared to be some significant linkages between government agencies and the university at the level of individual units and projects, the relationship between the university and government at the broader level seemed to have gone through some difficult times, and there were mixed views about this. On the one hand, according to one institutional leader, the university was usually the first choice for government when assistance was needed with policy development. In addition, many university academics were involved in the development of *Kenya Vision 2030* – from economics, sociology, political science and administration, amongst others. However, some respondents were quite sceptical about how the university was perceived by the government, claiming that academics were often accused of being too theoretical and not practical enough.

A number of respondents felt that there was still quite a residue of mistrust between the government and university, which was not always discussed openly, but which was certainly present. While academics did get co-opted into expert functions in certain policy areas, there was a sense that the 'knowledge industry' (of which the university is a central part) was not going to be allowed to drive the development process in the country. Mistrust also played itself out in the traditional autonomy tension where the university was subject to the State Corporations Act, which tended to be more restrictive than facilitative. There was a process underway to seek greater autonomy and strengthen the university's ability to determine its own direction and operations.

There were hardly any examples of linkages with the private sector or industry. The previous strategic plan referred to a study undertaken for the Commission for Higher Education which confirmed that relatively low collaboration exists between universities and industries in Kenya in relation to teaching and learning, as well as R&D initiatives.

There was a considerable amount of consultancy activities undertaken in the university and consultancy had been mainstreamed as a core function of the university. The University of Nairobi Enterprises and Services (UNES) Ltd was established in 1996, and had been considerably expanded, with the aim of promoting and coordinating the various income-generating activities of the university, including teaching, research and consultancy activities. UNES was registered as a private company, limited by shares, and operated as a separate legal entity, independent of the university.

Until recently, research activities in the university had gone largely uncoordinated. In particular, there was no institution-level unit responsible for coordinating research and much of the research that was done for outside organisations (e.g. government or donors) was negotiated by individuals within academic units. A positive development was that the Deans' Committee – essentially the university's research committee – established two research units (for the sciences and social sciences) which were responsible for coordinating research activities in their respective disciplinary areas. There were also plans to establish an office for a Deputy Vice Chancellor for Research and Development.

With regard to the connectedness of development-related activities to the academic core, the articulation and academic ratings applied to the six projects/centres are presented in Figure 6.

FIGURE 6 Plotting the development-related projects/centres at the University of Nairobi

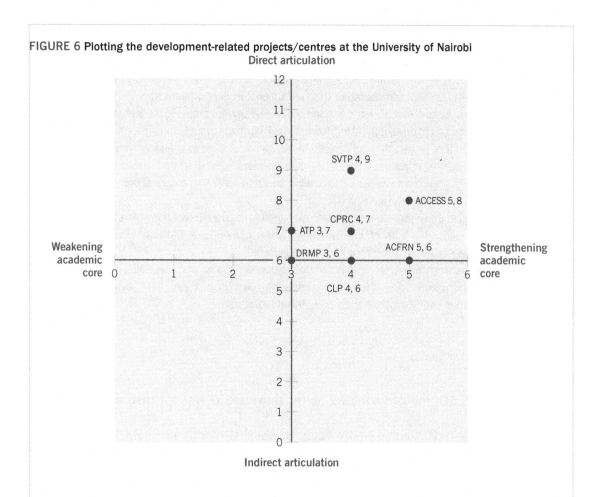

Key:

Abbreviation	Project/centre
ACCESS	African Collaborative Centre for Earth System Science
CPRC	Chronic Poverty Research Centre
ACFRN	African Clothing and Footwear Research Network
CLP	Child Labour Project
ATP	Applied Training Project
SVTP	Street Vendors and Traders Project
DRMP	Disaster and Risk Management Project

FINDINGS

- While there was evidence of connectedness between the university and industry or the private sector, these linkages were mostly confined to the level of units or centres rather than institutional-level partnerships.
- Projects/centres that were considered by university leadership to be strongly connected to development tended to score well on the articulation indicators – in other words, they reflected national priorities (and to a lesser extent institutional objectives), had more than one funding source and, in some cases, plans for financial sustainability, and may have had a connection to an implementation agency.
- Most of these projects/centres also managed to keep a strong connection to the academic core of the university, whilst others were somewhat disconnected from these core knowledge activities.
- There were 'exemplary' development projects/centres at the university. The problem was scale: there were simply not enough of these, and some seemed overly dependent on exceptional individuals.

7.5   Concluding comments about the Kenya/University of Nairobi case study

The *Kenya Vision 2030* is the new development blueprint covering the period 2008–2030. The main aim of the vision is to transform Kenya into a middle-income country. The anchors for this are macro-economic stability; governance reforms; enhanced equity and wealth creation; opportunities for the poor; infrastructure development; energy; and science, technology and innovation. This is supported by the Science, Technology and Innovation Bill (2009) whose point of departure is the promotion of research, science, technology and innovation for national socio-economic development.

Along with these promising developments are about a 6% GDP growth since 2007, a higher HDI than its neighbours, the third highest innovation capacity (after South Africa and Mauritius), and a relatively differentiated tertiary sector. While tertiary participation was still low, Kenya received relatively good ratings for quality of education and on-the-job training. However, the overall competitiveness potential was being eroded by a weakening of the institutional environment (moved down to 117 from 100 the previous year), government inefficiency (ranked 101) and rising corruption (116).

This picture of positive growth and a globalising vision for future development was undermined by a weakening institutional environment, a lack of policy coordination and implementation, and apparently weak steering towards very positive ideals. The lack of buy-in was reflected in the lack of concordance on the part of the University of Nairobi which, if not moving away from the knowledge economy vision, was certainly ambiguous about it and responding to it rather 'symbolically'. There was also still considerable mistrust from the side of the university and, as was asserted above, there was also not a strong, institutionalised interaction with business.

It is difficult not to conclude that despite a number of positives, and a very modern grand vision for the future, there was not a pact about the importance and the role of the university in development. Without a pact, and in a weakening institutional environment, it is not possible to do the necessary coordination and make the necessary trade-offs to redirect resources in order to implement the vision.

8
Mauritius and the University of Mauritius

8.1   The higher education and economic development context in Mauritius

How did Mauritius fare in meeting the 'preconditions' for an effective and productive relationship between higher education and economic development identified by Pillay's (2010b) investigation of three successful systems?

High-quality schooling: Participation rates were high at both the primary and secondary levels. However, there was considerable concern about inefficiencies in the system particularly around completion rates at the primary levels and quality of provision and outcomes throughout the system. The government had recognised that major efforts had to be made to ensure that quality was improved if Mauritius is to become a serious player in the knowledge economy.

Effective economic and education planning: There was no doubt that education planning attempts to move in tandem with economic planning. Serious efforts were being made to ensure that the tertiary education system was capable of producing the requisite magnitude and types of skills needed for a globalising and knowledge economy.

The role of the state: The state was playing an important role with respect to funding, encouraging private sector provision of higher education, and more recently in funding of R&D and innovation. The recent documents relating to research and innovation, and human resource development, suggested that the state would play a much more proactive role in ensuring that the tertiary education system moves sufficiently rapidly to meet the needs of the government's changing development strategy.

Partnerships: In general, partnerships between the universities and the private sector appeared to be at an early stage of development. It was encouraging to note that the government was putting in place funding initiatives to encourage such partnerships around research and innovation.

Institutional differentiation: In spite of being a relatively small system, there appeared to be considerable differentiation within the tertiary education system, with a university, a university of technology and a range of other post-secondary institutions as well as both public and private providers.

Quality: Serious questions had been raised about the quality of educational provision across the system. This problem had been recognised in government documents and efforts were being made to address it at all levels of the system.

Funding: State funding of tertiary education was relatively low in international and developing country terms. Some effort was being made to address the low levels of R&D funding but it was clear that much more needed to be done in this area if Mauritius was to compete effectively in the knowledge economy.

Innovation: At the time of the study, Mauritius had not invested sufficiently either in its universities or in its private sector, nor had it provided appropriate incentives for partnerships to develop between these two sets of important actors. There was little evidence outside pockets of excellence at the University of Mauritius to suggest any significant level in science and technology innovation or its diffusion.

8.2 Evidence of a pact around the role of higher education in Mauritius?

Mauritius's indicator ratings for the role of knowledge and universities in national and institutional policies and plans are presented in Table 25.

At the national level, of the eight countries under study, Mauritius was the most orientated towards investing in human capital formation and towards a knowledge economy as a key driver of development. In terms of the criteria used in this study to assess national governance and policy coordination, the concept of a knowledge economy featured strongly in Mauritius in their national development plan – as did the role for higher education in development in their national policies and plans.

Amongst the University of Mauritius leadership interviewed, there was agreement that the university's role was focussed on contributing to the development of the country. When the sugar industry was phased out and the attempted creation of an export processing zone did not take off, the university became, as knowledge provider, key in terms of addressing sectoral transformation. This required different faculties to revisit their programmes, courses and research agendas. Amongst the leadership there was a strong emphasis on knowledge, both for professional training and in terms of production and application.

Most interviewees commented on the important role played by the university over the years in producing highly skilled professionals for both the public and private sectors, and how links had been established with employers to aid in curriculum design. More recently, lifelong learning and continuous professional development had started receiving greater attention, as had developing an entrepreneurial flair amongst staff and students. The university was also trying to institutionalise its pool of intellectual resources which, through numerous advisory task teams and commissions, form part of many government think-tanks on national issues. None of the interviewees expressed a concern about institutional autonomy, or questioned the role of the university in relation to economic development.

TABLE 25 Role for knowledge and universities in development in Mauritius

National rating = 6/6			
The concept of a knowledge economy features in the national development plan	**3 Strong** Appears in a number of policies	2 Weak Only mentioned in one policy	1 Absent Not mentioned at all
A role for higher education in development in national policies and plans	**3 Prevalent** Clearly mentioned in development policies	2 Weak	1 Absent
University rating = 5/6			
Concept of a knowledge economy features in institutional policies and plans	**3** Features strongly in strategic plan and/or research policy/strategy	2 Vague reference in strategic plan or research policy	1 Not mentioned at all
Institutional policies with regard to the university's role in economic development	3 Institutional policy	**2** Embedded in strategic plan, research policy, etc.	1 No formal policies

FINDINGS

- There was strong agreement (pact) about a development model and the role of higher education in development, at both national and institutional levels.
- Mauritius was the only country and university in the sample that had accepted that knowledge, and by implication higher education, is key to development.
- The reconstitution of the ministry of education and higher education showed that Mauritius was actively trying to reorganise at the government level to achieve greater coordination towards their notion of a developmental state.
- There was awareness, and policies, about the importance of the knowledge economy approach across ministries.

Notions of the role of knowledge and universities in development

Table 26 summarises the notions of the role of higher education held by national and institutional stakeholders, and indicates whether the notion was strong, prevalent, present or absent altogether.

While acknowledging that there is seldom a single notion about the role of higher education, at the University of Mauritius there was a very strong emphasis in both the interviews and the key planning and strategy documents that the university must be connected, through its role as the knowledge institution, to national development. The knowledge economy notion ran concurrent with that of the instrument for development notion but, interestingly, the latter was directed at government and business, while there was very little mention of linkages to communities.

TABLE 26 Comparing national and institutional notions of the role of higher education in Mauritius

Notions	National stakeholders		University stakeholders	
Ancillary	•	No ancillary notion	•	The university was never seen as being inactive in national development
Self-governing	☐	Readily acknowledge autonomy, but with strong contribution to development discourse	☐	For as long as anybody can remember the university was seen as having an active role in development
Instrument for development agendas	◼	Only complaint is that university can do more, and more relevant, activities	☐	Very instrumental, with the university regarded as being important in solving a range of societal problems
Engine for development	◼	Dominant policy discourse	◼	More than an orientation, it is the dominant discourse

Key:

◼ Strong ☐ Present • Absent

FINDINGS

- In terms of notions of the role of the university in development, at the national level and at the institutional level there was agreement about the engine of development notion.
- At the national level there was some dissatisfaction that the university was not doing enough to contribute to development, but this was sometimes mixed with a rather more traditional instrumentalist notion.
- At the institutional level, the main dissatisfaction was that government was not supportive enough for the academics to contribute more towards development.

8.3 The academic core of the University of Mauritius

The analysis of the university's academic core presented in the case study report was undertaken on the basis of the rating of seven key indicators as 'strong', 'medium' or 'weak'. The data on which the ratings are based are contained in the detailed case study report.[19] The seven indicators and their ratings are presented in Table 27.

---

19   The Mauritius and University of Mauritius case study report is available at www.chet.org.za.

TABLE 27 **University of Mauritius: Rating of the academic core**

Indicator		Rating (strong/medium/weak)*
1	Science, engineering and technology enrolments and graduations	SET students = 42% in 2007. 26% of students expected to graduate
2	Postgraduate/undergraduate enrolments ratio Masters/PhD enrolment ratio	Proportion of postgraduates at 13% for 2001–2007. PhD enrolments as % of masters and doctoral enrolments = 18% in 2007
3	Teaching load: Academic staff–student ratio	Overall ratio at 1:16 (2007). SET ratio not available
4	Proportion of academic staff with doctorates	45% of permanent academics have doctorates (2007)
5	Research income per permanent academic staff member**	Low at PPP$ 3 000
6	Doctoral graduates	Graduates in 2007 constituted 5% of permanent academics
7	Research publications	Outputs in 2007 were 0.13 of publications per permanent academic

Key:

■ Strong ▦ Medium □ Weak

* Refer to Appendix F for a detailed descriptions of the academic core rating categories.

** The research income data are based on the university's report on income from research contracts.

The following observations can be made about the academic core data for the University of Mauritius:

1. **SET enrolments**: The university's SET enrolments grew slowly from 2 700 in 2001 to 3 100 in 2007. Most of the growth occurred in the field of business and management, where enrolments doubled from 1 200 in 2001 to 2 400 in 2007. The proportion of SET students remained high (at 42%) in 2007. The SET graduation rate was relatively high compared to other universities in the sample.

2. **Increased postgraduate enrolments**: The university's total enrolment of postgraduate students grew from 9% in 2001 to 14% in 2007. It reported rapid growth in masters enrolments as well as masters graduates. Masters enrolments (not including MPhils) increased from 350 in 2001 to 859 in 2007 (an average annual increase of 16.1%). Masters graduates increased from 79 in 2001 to 360 in 2007 (an average annual increase of 28.2%). A point which must be noted is that the university reported its senior postgraduate enrolments as MPhil/doctorates, with the decision on the final track of a student being taken during his/her research studies. What was a concern was that very few of these joint MPhil/doctoral students appeared to move into full doctoral studies. The university produced an annual average of only seven doctoral graduates between 2001 and 2007.

3. **Teaching load**: The university's FTE academic staff more than doubled the growth in FTE student enrolment. As a consequence, its FTE student to FTE academic staff ratio fell from 24:1 in 2001 to 16:1 in 2007. This improvement was the result of the university employing a considerable number of temporary and part-time academics in 2007. Its permanent academic total was 201 in 2007 and its FTE academic staff

total 411. This shows that the university's permanent academics must, by 2007, have had reasonable teaching loads.

4. **Qualifications of staff**: In 2007, 45% of the university's permanent academic staff had doctorates as their highest formal qualifications.

5. **Research funding**: The university indicated that its income from research contracts was Rs 9.3 million in 2007, which was 2.5% of its total income. This amount was equivalent to USD 300 000 at market exchange rates and in purchasing power parity units, PPP$ 600 000. These converted sums, when divided by the university's total of permanent academics become: USD 1 500 per academic and PPP$ 3 000 per academic. These ratios, compared to the amounts available to South African universities which are strong in research, were low and suggest that the university may not have been able to adequately fund its research activities.

6. **Doctoral graduates**: Between 2001 and 2007, doctoral graduates increased by 6%. However, this was coming off a low base of only seven. This resulted in the very low ratio of 2.8% of doctoral graduates to permanent academic staff.

7. **Research publications**: The university's research publications output was low. Its 2007 ratio of publication units per permanent academic was, at 0.13, well below the ratio of 0.50 which had been set as a target for South Africa's research universities.

On the input side, the university was strong in SET enrolments and increases in postgraduate enrolments. It had also managed to decrease the staff teaching load through the appointment of part-time staff, which shifted the workload to administration of part-timers. The qualifications of staff were above the average for South African universities.

The main input weakness seemed to be lack of research funds, which presumably impacted on the weak outputs in doctoral graduates and research publications. It also seemed that the university would have to do a serious rethink of incentives if it wanted to become a knowledge producer that can contribute significantly to an engine of development approach.

FINDINGS

*   The knowledge production output variables of the academic core did not seem strong enough to enable the university to make a sustainable contribution to development.
*   The university was not changing significantly from a predominantly undergraduate teaching institution, with a strength in SET and business studies, to a research institution.
*   On the input side, the university scored strongly on SET graduations, but weak on doctoral graduates and publications.
*   The most serious challenges to strengthening the academic core seemed to be to increase research funding, doctoral graduation rates and research outputs.

8.4 Coordination and connectedness

Knowledge policy coordination and implementation in Mauritius

Table 28 presents the ratings for the coordination of knowledge policies at the national level. There was effective planning between state organs responsible for development planning and those responsible for tertiary education. With regard to the latter, without resorting to any form of 'manpower planning', the nature of planning in the education sectors suggested attempts to ensure the provision of generic skills and improving the quality of outcomes. However, there were no formal structures linking national authorities and higher education institutions.

TABLE 28 National coordination of knowledge policies in Mauritius

National rating = 7/9			
Economic development and higher education planning are linked	**3 Systematic** Formal structures Headed by senior minister	2 Sporadic Clusters/forums	1 Weak Occasional meetings
Link between universities and national authorities	3 Specific coordination structures or agencies	**2** Some formal structures but no meaningful coordination	1 No structures, and political rather than professional networks
Coordination and consensus building of government agencies involved in higher education	3 Higher education mainstreamed across government departments	**2** Intermittent interaction with ineffective forums	1 Higher education issues limited mainly to one ministry or directorate

FINDINGS

- At the national level, there were considerable coordination activities, including clusters and the reorganisation of the national ministry.
- While there were many personal networks between government officials and particular university leaders, which contributed to a shared understanding about the university's role in development (pact), the question is whether these were contributing towards strengthening the sector.

Table 29 summarises the ratings of the indicators relating to the implementation of knowledge policies and activities at both the national and university levels.

TABLE 29 Implementation of knowledge policies and activities in Mauritius

National rating = 8/12			
Role of the ministry responsible for higher education	3 Organised ministry with capacity to make predictable allocations	**2** Spots of capacity with some steering instruments	1 Weak capacity with unpredictable allocations
Implementation to 'steer' higher education towards development	3 Strong Instruments such as funding/ special projects that incentivise institutions/individuals	**2 Weak** Occasional grants for special projects	1 Absent No particular incentive funding
Balance/ratio of sources of income for institutions	3 Government, fees and third stream	**2** Mainly government plus student fees	1 Mainly government with external funders
Funding consistency*	3 A stable, transparent public funding mechanism based on criteria agreed upon by all actors involved	**2** Funding allocations somewhat predictable but do not allow for long-term planning nor reward enterprising behaviour	1 No clear funding or incentives from government
University rating = 13/18			
Specific units, funding or appointments linked to economic development	**3** Specific units, funding or appointments	2 Economic development initiatives aspect of a unit or appointment	1 Mainly ad hoc, staff-initiated operations
Incentives and rewards for development-related activities	3 Incentives/counts towards promotion	2 Some signals but largely rhetoric	**1** No mention
Teaching programmes linked to the labour market	3 Targets for enrolments in fields considered to be of high economic relevance	**2** Some programmes in response to specific industry requests	1 No new programmes linked to labour market
Special programmes linking students to economic development	**3** Entrepreneurship, work-based learning and/or incubators for students mainstreamed	2 Ad hoc programmes	1 No special programmes
Research activities are becoming more economy-oriented	**3** Research policy/strategy has an economic development focus	2 Some research agendas have an economic development focus	1 Ad hoc project funding
Levels of government and institutional funding for research	3 High	2 Medium	**1** Low

* Our original rating for funding consistency was '2'. However, since the collection of data for this case study, it came to light that the way in which tertiary education institutions are funded ('programme-based budgeting') does allow for some degree of long-term planning on the part of institutions.

FINDINGS

- At the national level, one of the weaknesses was implementation of new policies, particularly those that require a shift of resources. In addition, while there were some steering instruments and mechanisms, these did not seem strong enough to 'redirect' the system.
- While the university did have development-related structures and special programmes linking it to development initiatives, the problem was that in too many cases these initiatives were driven by individuals rather than being institutionalised. In addition, these special implementation efforts need to be more connected.
- Despite policies that extol the importance of research related to development activities (mainly through focus themes), research related to development was not rewarded through incentives beyond the traditional academic promotion system.

The University of Mauritius's connectedness to external stakeholders and the academic core

A number of institutional stakeholders reported that there were good linkages between government and university academics. The university's *Strategic and Research and Innovation Framework* uses the 'triple-helix' model to frame linkages and collaboration with government and industry. Key mechanisms for the transfer of technology to government and industry included consultancy services, outright sale of technology, licensing of technology, joint ventures, and start-up ventures. Consultancy projects included research projects, routine testing in the university's laboratories, training programmes, executive development programmes, and continuous development programmes.

There was a serious attempt to institutionalise collaboration through establishing various parks (e.g. science and technology, industrial, research), as well as structures such as Enterprise Mauritius, the Mauritius National Productivity and Competitiveness Council, and the Small Enterprises and Handicraft Development Authority – all of which were involved in entrepreneurship or innovation in one way or another. However, two serious shortcomings were raised: firstly, that government did not draw adequately on the expertise of the academics and, secondly, that there was poor coordination between the key stakeholders. A number of respondents suggested in different ways that the interactions were ad hoc and that often particular government departments were not interested in utilising data and findings from development-orientated projects. The considerable research and innovation infrastructure was not systematically coordinated amongst the different initiatives. Even the Centre for Consultancy and Contract Research at the University of Mauritius, which was established to provide greater coordination between internal and external interests, was reported to be largely uncoordinated.

At the university, there was considerable private sector involvement in curriculum review and development, and work placements. However, a number of respondents felt that the scale of work placements was not large enough. It has already been mentioned that there was little private sector investment in R&D, and that it happened in an ad hoc manner. Two university leaders argued that there was no existing coordinating body; however, it was mentioned there were plans for a university–industry liaison body. It was also mentioned that linkages with the university and government, and particularly the university and industry, would be enhanced with greater staff exchange. It was certainly noticeable for the research team that links with government and development projects were much stronger with academics that had been seconded to government for limited period-specific projects. With regard to the connectedness of development-related activities to the academic core, the articulation and academic ratings applied to the six projects/centres are presented in Figure 7.

FIGURE 7 Plotting the development-related projects/centres at the University of Mauritius

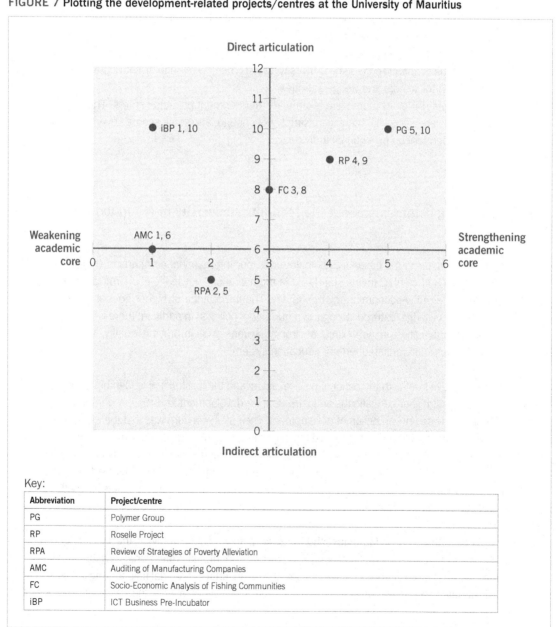

Key:

Abbreviation	Project/centre
PG	Polymer Group
RP	Roselle Project
RPA	Review of Strategies of Poverty Alleviation
AMC	Auditing of Manufacturing Companies
FC	Socio-Economic Analysis of Fishing Communities
iBP	ICT Business Pre-Incubator

FINDINGS

- While there was evidence of connectedness between the university and industry or the private sector, these linkages were mostly confined to the level of units or centres rather than institutional-level partnerships.
- Unlike most of the universities in the sample, the University of Mauritius was involved in a wide array of R&D consultancies with, or for, industry.
- Projects/centres that were considered by university leadership to be strongly connected to development tended to score well on the articulation indicators – in other words, they reflected national priorities (and to a lesser extent institutional objectives), had more than one funding source and, in some cases, plans for financial sustainability, and may have had a connection to an implementation agency.
- Some of these projects/centres also managed to keep a strong connection to the academic core of the university, whilst others were quite disconnected from these core knowledge activities.
- At the university there were 'exemplary' development projects/centres. The problem was scale: there were simply not enough, and some seemed overly dependent on exceptional individuals.

8.5 Concluding comments about the Mauritius/University of Mauritius case study

Mauritius, similar to the case studies included in our international comparison (Finland, South Korea and North Carolina state), made the notion of 'knowledge economy' a strong feature of their new economic growth strategy. The importance of higher education and high-level knowledge featured strongly in a number of policies. In addition, there were high levels of participation in schooling, a strong awareness of improving quality, and an expanding and differentiated tertiary education system.

At the narrative level both the national political actors and the institutional leadership shared the notion that higher education is an instrument for development and the key component of their knowledge-driven notion of development. Their main concern was that the expertise of the academic staff is not yet applied efficiently enough. On the side of the academics there was frustration that they were not given enough incentives and rewards to fulfil a knowledge production and innovation role. Neither the government, nor the institutional leadership, regarded the university as a luxury, and there were no apparent autonomy conflicts. On both sides the concerns were about not delivering on the broadly agreed upon goals.

Within the University of Mauritius, the strategic plan reflected many of the knowledge economy notions. For example, lifelong learning and continuous professional development were receiving more attention, as well as developing an 'entrepreneurial flair' amongst staff and students which was described in both the strategic plan and the research and innovation strategy. There were also special academic programmes attempting to provide students with appropriate labour market knowledge skills through work–based learning, participation in incubators and entrepreneurship courses.

Apart from establishing structures such as the Office of the Pro-Vice-Chancellor Research and Innovation, five research clusters had been identified to concentrate research focus and resources. However, while research activities were becoming increasingly economy orientated, it seemed that government funding for research remained very low, and was becoming more difficult to access. The internal incentive/reward structure of the institution had also not changed to reflect the new direction. It could be argued that the pact was not strong enough to enable the government to make the necessary trade-offs to allocate more resources to the knowledge project, and the same applies within the institution. And there was little financial support from industry or external funders.

What does the academic core of the university tell us about the 'state of knowledge'? Mauritius had a relatively high enrolment and graduation in SET, and there was substantial growth in postgraduate enrolment, but not in doctoral graduation. The teaching load was quite favourable, if somewhat inefficient, and the permanent staff were well-qualified, but the production of knowledge according to publication output, was very low. Funding for research was very low, and seemed to be getting more, and not less, difficult to access. Despite the positives mentioned, unless there is a stronger PhD output (producing a cadre of possible researchers), and a substantial increase in research resources and productivity, the University of Mauritius will find it very difficult to operationalise its knowledge economy ambitions.

The national education department had some capacity to facilitate interaction, but it seemed that this role was increasingly fulfilled by the Tertiary Education Commission. As was the case in so many other countries, the department of education was not strong in the hierarchy of government departments, and was thus restricted in terms of the steering/ coordinating role it could play.

However, it did seem that neither amongst government departments, nor between government and university, was there strong formal coordination. A number of respondents suggested in different ways that the interactions between the government and the university community were more ad hoc than systematic, and that often particular government departments were not interested in utilising data and findings from development-orientated projects. A corollary complaint was that government did not draw adequately on the expertise of the academics.

The university had made considerable progress in institutionalising development projects. Within the university a number of dedicated posts, units and centres (particularly the Centre for Consultancy and Contract Research) had been established to improve coordination and ensure sustainability. Key mechanisms for the transfer of technology to government and industry included consultancy services, outright sale of technology, licensing of technology, joint ventures and start-up ventures, executive development programmes and continuous development programmes. Consultancy projects included research projects, routine testing in the university's laboratories, and training programmes.

The very ambitious science and technology park was probably the largest attempt to coordinate and institutionalise research and consultancy projects. Also in the pipeline, in addition to structures such as Enterprise Mauritius, Small Enterprises and Handicraft Authority, was the attempt to establish a formal university–industry council.

Not only had certain teaching programmes been established to respond to labour market needs, but formal curriculum consultation committees and processes had been established across the University of Mauritius to improve labour market linkage.

Much of the emphasis in the university's key planning and strategy documents was on the institution's relationship with industry and government, with very little mention of linkages to communities – indicating that the university sees its development role as a triangle with government and industry. This was interestingly reflected in the six development-related projects included in the study – all had strong and direct articulation between project aims and national priorities. However, this was not the case in terms of articulation with institutional objectives where three of the projects did not report any direct linkages. It is perhaps not surprising that two of these projects were once-off consultancy projects which were initiated by external agencies.

In terms of connectedness to external stakeholders, five of the six projects had either direct or indirect links with implementation agencies – and most of these projects were initiated and funded by external agencies.

While there is no doubt that the six projects in various ways made important contributions to development in their field of expertise, particularly in the application of expertise, the overall low ratings for contributions to strengthening the academic core is worrying since this is the main business of the university. And, according to our analytical framework, suggests that it inhibits the university's potential to make a significant and sustained contribution to development.

In conclusion, both government and intuitional leaders had a strong knowledge economy discourse and an impressive array of policies in place. The coordination of these policies was still a major problem, and the pact did not seem strong enough for government to make resource trade-offs to support this vision; nor had the university managed to strengthen its academic core sufficiently to shift from a rather traditional teaching institution to a knowledge producing and innovation institution. The fundamental challenge facing Mauritius at the time of the study was that while it had enthusiastically adopted the notion of a knowledge economy in most of its policies, the University of Mauritius did not seem yet to be in a position to produce the knowledge to operationalise this new vision.

9

Mozambique and the
Eduardo Mondlane University

9.1 The higher education and economic development context in Mozambique

How did Mozambique fare in meeting the 'preconditions' for an effective and productive relationship between higher education and economic development identified by Pillay's (2010b) investigation of three successful systems?

High-quality schooling: Participation rates were relatively low at both the primary and secondary levels. The net enrolment ratio in primary education increased significantly from 52% in 1999 to 76% in 2006, but still left the country far short of achieving universal primary education. The secondary schooling participation rates were shocking and illustrate very clearly why Mozambique has been unable to build a sound foundation for an effective tertiary education system. In 2006, the gross enrolment ratio in secondary schooling was 16% and the net enrolment ratio was 4% (UNESCO 2009). The corresponding averages for sub-Saharan Africa were 32% and 25%, not high by developing country standards (60% and 53%, respectively), but much higher than the Mozambique figures. Moreover, there was considerable concern about inefficiencies in the system particularly around completion rates at the primary levels and quality of provision and outcomes throughout the system. The survival rate to the last grade of primary schooling was 40% in 2006 (the average for sub-Saharan Africa was 67% and that for developing countries, 81%) (ibid.).

Effective economic and education planning: A serious commitment to economic and education planning was reflected in the policy documents. However, there was little evidence that such planning was actually taking place.

The role of the state: The state (through donor funding) was playing an important role with respect to funding, as well as encouraging private sector provision of higher education. The state's policy documents gave prominence to the role of tertiary education in development; however, financial resource constraints had clearly prevented it from ensuring effective implementation of desired policies.

Partnerships: In general, no evidence could be gleaned of partnerships between the state, the universities and the private sector.

Institutional differentiation: There was evidence of differentiation amongst universities (e.g. Eduardo Mondlane University vs. the Pedagogic University) and across the system (universities vs. polytechnics). It is likely also that most of the research and innovation was taking place at Eduardo Mondlane and that the other higher education institutions were forced, because of a lack of financial and human resources, to focus largely on their education and training function.

Quality: Serious questions had been raised about the quality of educational provision across the system. The finding on poor quality features prominently in the WEF's Global Competitiveness Index and Global Innovation Index.

Funding: State funding of tertiary education was low in absolute terms given the extent of need and the imperative to increase access and enhance equity.

Innovation: At the time of the study, Mozambique had not invested sufficiently either in its universities or its private sector, nor had it provided appropriate incentives for partnerships to develop between these two sets of important actors.

9.2 Evidence of a pact around the role of higher education in Mozambique?

Mozambique's indicator ratings for the role of knowledge and universities in national and institutional policies and plans are presented in Table 30.

At the national level, there was strong policy commitment to both the knowledge economy and a strong role for higher education in development. At the institutional level, while there was a commitment to science, research and innovation at the level of discourse amongst the top leadership, it was not reflected in the university's strategic plan; neither were there any formal structures or funding incentives to promote it.

TABLE 30 Role for knowledge and universities in development in Mozambique

National rating = 5/6			
The concept of a knowledge economy features in the national development plan	3 Strong Appears in a number of policies	**2 Weak** Only mentioned in one policy	1 Absent Not mentioned at all
A role for higher education in development in national policies and plans	**3 Prevalent** Clearly mentioned in development policies	2 Weak	1 Absent
University rating = 3/6			
Concept of a knowledge economy features in institutional policies and plans	3 Features strongly in strategic plan and/or research policy/strategy	**2** Vague reference in strategic plan or research policy	1 Not mentioned at all
Institutional policies with regard to the university's role in economic development	3 Institutional policy	2 Embedded in strategic plan, research policy, etc.	**1** No formal policies

FINDINGS

- At the national level, the importance of the knowledge economy was only mentioned in one policy. However, the importance of higher education in development was clearly mentioned in a number of policy statements.
- In contrast, at the institutional level, there was a weaker reference to the knowledge economy and the important role of the university in development was not mentioned in the strategic plan.
- There was no broad agreement between the national and institutional levels that knowledge, and by implication higher education, is key to development.

Notions of the role of knowledge and universities in development

Table 31 summarises the notions of the role of higher education held by national and institutional stakeholders, and indicates whether the notion was strong, prevalent, present or absent altogether.

While acknowledging that all four notions would be present within most universities, the question is: what appears to be the dominant discourse during a particular period amongst the key national and institutional stakeholders? It appeared that while there was still quite a strong belief that the university as an institution was important in national development, in producing professionals for government and industry, and in producing scientific knowledge, there was no need for a *direct* role in national development. This was reflected in the repeated reference to the core functions of teaching, research and service. This self-governing notion was accompanied by both an instrumental and an engine of development discourse, with the latter stronger in government than in the university, but with very little operationalisation.

TABLE 31 Comparing national and institutional notions of the role of higher education in Mozambique

Notions		National stakeholders		University stakeholders
Ancillary	▫	Want higher education more involved in development	▫	See the university as central to development
Self-governing	☐	Autonomy is accepted, but there is strong political involvement	■	A strong traditional notion of teaching-research-service
Instrument for development agendas	■	Wants stronger direct service provision by academic experts	☐	There is a discourse of delivering more service, but no incentives
Engine for development	☐	Strong discourse, but not in policy or implementation	▫	Weaker in discourse than government, and not even reflected in official policies

Key:

■ Strong   ☐ Present   ▫ Absent

FINDINGS

- In terms of notions of the role of the university in development, at the national level there was a strong instrumental expectation, with some reference to the autonomy issue.
- At the institutional level, there was a strong leaning towards the self-governing notion, with constant reference to instrumental, although the latter was not dominant.
- At both the national and the institutional levels the instrumental and self-governing notions were prevalent, but not resolved. Amongst university leadership there was a much weaker discourse about the engine of development approach.

9.3   The academic core of the Eduardo Mondlane University

The analysis of the university's academic core presented in the case study report was undertaken on the basis of the rating of seven key indicators as 'strong', 'medium' or 'weak'. The data on which the ratings are based are contained in the detailed case study report.[20] The seven indicators and their ratings are presented in Table 32.

TABLE 32 Eduardo Mondlane University: Rating of the academic core

	Indicator	Rating (strong/medium/weak)*
1	Science, engineering and technology enrolments and graduations	SET majors have 47% enrolment share, but graduation rate is far too low (2007)
2	Postgraduate/undergraduate enrolments ratio Masters/PhD enrolment ratio	Postgraduates = 4% of enrolments in 2007 Masters output low, and no doctoral enrolments until 2006
3	Teaching load: Academic staff–student ratio	Overall and SET FTE student: academic ratio both = 13:1 (2007) Business ratio problematic at 50:1
4	Proportion of academic staff with doctorates	24% of academics with doctorates
5	Research income per permanent academic staff member**	Reported no research income for 2007
6	Doctoral graduates	Graduates in 2007 constituted 0.00% of permanent academics
7	Research publications	Research productivity poor with 0.04% in 2001 and 2007 Very few academics publish research articles.

Key:

■ Strong   ▨ Medium   ☐ Weak

* Refer to Appendix F for a detailed descriptions of the academic core rating categories.

** The research income data are based on the university's 2007 financial statements which indicated that research funding = 0.

---

20   The Mozambique and Eduardo Mondlane University case study report is available at www.chet.org.za.

The following observations can be made about the academic core data for the Eduardo Mondlane University:

1. **SET enrolments**: The university's SET enrolments grew from 4 500 in 2001 to 7 600 in 2007. The average annual SET growth rate was 9.1% over this period, which was below the growth rate in other fields of study. Because of the differences in growth rates, the proportion of SET students fell from 62% in 2001 to 47% in 2007. This was still a good proportion, but it was off-set by the university's very poor SET graduation rate. Its output ratios suggest that only about 20 of every 100 students entering the SET programmes would eventually graduate.

2. **Postgraduate enrolments**: The university's proportion of postgraduate students in its total enrolment was low, and remained low, throughout this period. It enrolled masters students for the first time in 2002 and doctoral students for the first time in 2006. In 2007, its masters enrolment was 602 and its doctoral enrolment only three. The postgraduate students constituted 4% of the total enrolment in 2007.

3. **Teaching load**: Between 2001 and 2007, the university's FTE academic staff total grew at half the average annual growth rate of FTE students. As a consequence, its FTE student to FTE academic staff ratio increased from 9:1 in 2001 to 13:1 in 2007. Its 2007 ratio could, nevertheless, be regarded as a satisfactory one, in comparison to the South African norm of 20:1. The university increased its teaching staff capacity by about 20% in 2007 through the employment of temporary and part-time academic staff. The conclusion which can be drawn is that its permanent academics must, in 2007, have had reasonable teaching loads.

4. **Qualifications of staff**: In 2007, 24% of the university's permanent academic staff had doctorates as their highest formal qualifications. This proportion was below the average for South African universities.

5. **Research funding**: The estimates calculated suggest that the university did not have designated funds available to support the research activities of its academic staff.

6. **Doctoral graduates**: In 2007, the university only had three doctoral enrolments and no graduates. Historically, doctoral studies were undertaken abroad.

7. **Research publications**: In terms of research publications, the university's output was extremely low. In 2007, its 842 permanent staff produced only 21 research articles.

In terms of input variables, the university had a strong enrolment in SET and a very positive student–staff ratio. However, there were low postgraduate enrolments (although masters enrolments improved from 0 in 2001 to 420 in 2007), the lowest staff qualifications in the sample, and very little research funding per permanent academic staff member. SET graduation and knowledge production outputs were also the weakest in the sample. Positive developments were the increase in masters students, and the beginnings of enrolling PhDs.

FINDINGS

- The university was not changing from a predominantly undergraduate teaching institution.
- On the input side, the university scored strongly on two indicators, namely SET enrolments and staff teaching load, and scored weak on all three output indicators.
- The knowledge production output variables of the academic core did not seem strong enough to enable the university to make a sustainable contribution to development.

9.4   Coordination and connectedness

Knowledge policy coordination and implementation

Table 33 presents the ratings for the coordination of knowledge policies at the national level. Acknowledging a lack of coordination within government, and between government and the university, two national bodies were established to serve as forums for interaction between government, universities and civil society. One was the Higher Education Council which brings together the university, civil society and other actors such as representatives of the Ministry of Finance. The other was the Council on Science and Technology which involved the rectors of some of the universities as well as civil society representatives. In order to pull these different groups together, a National Council for Higher Education, Science and Technology was established, reporting directly to the Council of Ministers. However, it appeared that this body had never really functioned properly. For instance, one interview respondent commented that when this Council met, it was apparent that the parties did not know each other and that there was no coordination and an overlap in some activities. This highlights the importance of having both horizontal and vertical dialogue. In addition, while forums between higher education and government, and in some cases civil society, are becoming quite widespread in Africa, there is seldom follow-through or monitoring of implementation of decisions. Instead, these forums often create a diversionary illusion of consultation and coordination.

TABLE 33 National coordination of knowledge policies in Mozambique

National rating = 4/9			
Economic development and higher education planning are linked	3 Systematic Formal structures Headed by senior minister	2 Sporadic Clusters/forums	**1 Weak** Occasional meetings
Link between universities and national authorities	3 Specific coordination structures or agencies	**2** Some formal structures but no meaningful coordination	1 No structures, and political rather than professional networks
Coordination and consensus building of government agencies involved in higher education	3 Higher education mainstreamed across government departments	2 Intermittent interaction with ineffective forums	**1** Higher education issues limited mainly to one ministry or directorate

FINDINGS

- At the national level, there seemed to be mainly informal interactions, but no institutionalised processes of coordination.
- While there were considerable personal networks between government officials and particular university leaders, it was not clear whether these were contributing towards building consensus and strengthening the institution.
- When it comes to structures, resources and incentives – in other words implementation – there was weak capacity in the ministry; there had been only one serious steering attempt. There was also funding inconsistency.

Table 34 summarises the ratings of the indicators relating to the implementation of knowledge policies and activities at both the national and university levels.

TABLE 34 Implementation of knowledge policies and activities in Mozambique

National rating = 5/12			
Role of the ministry responsible for higher education	3 Organised ministry with capacity to make predictable allocations	2 Spots of capacity with some steering instruments	**1** Weak capacity with unpredictable allocations
Implementation to 'steer' higher education towards development	3 Strong Instruments such as funding/special projects that incentivise institutions/ individuals	2 Weak Occasional grants for special projects	**1 Absent** No particular incentive funding
Balance/ratio of sources of income for institutions	3 Government, fees and third stream	2 Mainly government plus student fees	**1** Mainly government with external funders
Funding consistency	3 A stable, transparent public funding mechanism based on criteria agreed upon by all actors involved	**2** Funding allocations somewhat predictable but do not allow for long-term planning nor reward enterprising behaviour	1 No clear funding or incentives from government
University rating = 7/18			
Specific units, funding or appointments linked to economic development	3 Specific units, funding or appointments	2 Economic development initiatives aspect of a unit or appointment	**1** Mainly ad hoc, staff-initiated operations
Incentives and rewards for development-related activities	3 Incentives/counts towards promotion	**2** Some signals but largely rhetoric	1 No mention
Teaching programmes linked to the labour market	3 Targets for enrolments in fields considered to be of high economic relevance	2 Some programmes in response to specific industry requests	**1** No new programmes linked to labour market
Special programmes linking students to economic development	3 Entrepreneurship, work-based learning and/or incubators for students mainstreamed	2 Ad hoc programmes	**1** No special programmes
Research activities becoming more economy-oriented	3 Research policy/strategy has an economic development focus	2 Some research agendas have an economic development focus	**1** Ad hoc project funding
Levels of government and institutional funding for research	3 High	2 Medium	**1** Low

FINDINGS

- At the national level, the Department of Education seemed to have low capacity with no steering mechanisms and somewhat unpredictable funding.
- The university had a few development-related structures linking it to development initiatives. The problem was that most of these were driven by individuals rather than being institutionalised.
- Research related to development was not significantly rewarded through incentives beyond the traditional academic promotion system and foreign consultancies.

The Eduardo Mondlane University's connectedness to external stakeholders and the academic core

At the institutional level, there was little evidence of interactions with industry and the private sector – perhaps in part because these sectors were not well developed in Mozambique. There were also no real incentives for academics to engage in research or engagement activities, let alone those linked specifically to economic development. Instead, the increased pressure to expand access and the diversion of a proliferation of private institutions that offer salary supplementation to academics at the public institutions, was a strong disincentive for R&D activities.

Regarding coordination, there was a long tradition and practice of coordinating linkages with foreign donors. Over and above the support received from the World Bank via the government, one of the university's biggest donor partners had been SIDA/SAREC – with which the institution has had a more than 30-year relationship. Over the years, SIDA had funded individual projects, capacity development (including masters and PhD degrees), bigger research programmes, and a facilities fund which covers expensive equipment and the maintenance of laboratories and so on. Over the past few years, it had been mandatory to include masters and PhD training in the larger research programmes funded by SIDA.

There were systems in place to negotiate with the larger donors (such as from Sweden, Italy and Belgium) that the programmes that were funded were aligned with both institutional and national priorities. This was coordinated by the newly established Donor Coordination Unit. However, it was much more difficult to ensure this with the smaller donor-funded projects since these were usually negotiated with individual researchers. The Donor Coordination Unit, which reports directly to the vice-chancellor, would also be responsible for bringing together the major donors to meet and discuss their activities in order to coordinate funding areas and reporting mechanisms, and to avoid duplication or overlap where possible. The unit's coordinator reported that at a recent meeting of large donors, it was evident that there was little coordination between them in terms of funding areas and activities. This was certainly the most structured level of donor coordination we had seen in the eight country case studies.

With regard to the connectedness of development-related activities to the academic core, the articulation and academic ratings applied to the five projects/centres are presented in Figure 8.

FIGURE 8 Plotting the development-related projects/centres at the Eduardo Mondlane University

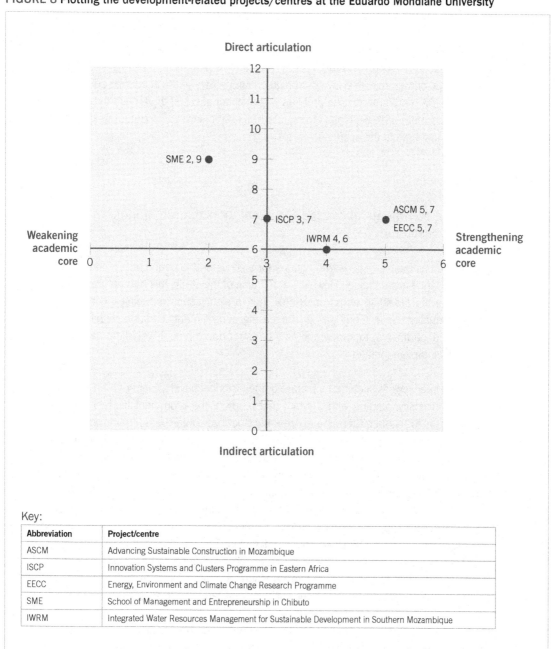

Key:

Abbreviation	Project/centre
ASCM	Advancing Sustainable Construction in Mozambique
ISCP	Innovation Systems and Clusters Programme in Eastern Africa
EECC	Energy, Environment and Climate Change Research Programme
SME	School of Management and Entrepreneurship in Chibuto
IWRM	Integrated Water Resources Management for Sustainable Development in Southern Mozambique

FINDINGS

- Projects/centres that were considered by university leadership to be strongly connected to development tended to score well on the articulation indicators – in other words, they reflected national priorities (and to a lesser extent institutional objectives), had more than one funding source and, in some cases, plans for financial sustainability, and may have had a connection to an implementation agency.
- Three of the projects also scored high on strengthening the academic core (a SIDA requirement). The problem was a matter of scale: there need to be many more of these types of projects which articulate development goals and strengthen the academic core.

9.5 Concluding comments about the Mozambique/Eduardo Mondlane University case study

Mozambique has been a high growth country for a considerable period and is often cited as a 'World Bank success case'. However, at the time of the study, this had not translated into climbing the ladder in terms of its HDI, nor in significantly reducing income and regional inequality. While there was an increasing commitment, certainly within some government departments, to knowledge as a basis for development, very little had been done to effect implementation.

Some of the interviewees sketched a picture of the historical development of the Eduardo Mondlane University, starting with the fact that many of the prominent leaders – from Samora Machel to Joaquim Chissano to Armando Guebuza – interrupted their own higher education studies in order to join the struggle for liberation, although retaining a strong appreciation for the power of knowledge. The university developed from a predominantly teaching institution, through the temporary closure following independence, to the introduction of research into the core activities in the 1980s. During the 1990s the Presidential Forum on Science and Technology, and President Chissano's (1997) national commission, led very appropriately by the Minister for Economic and Social Affairs, resulted in the establishment of the Ministry of Higher Education, Science and Technology. The first national science and technology policy was developed and approved in 2003 – the first real attempt to steer the system in the direction of science and technology, and a demonstration that the government recognised its importance in development.

The university responded positively by, amongst others, incorporating smaller projects into new, bigger programmes which were evaluated according to their contribution to national priorities, such as the government's poverty alleviation strategy. This signalled some alignment between the university's research policy and the priorities of the Mozambique Science, Technology and Innovation Strategy.

But, alas, according to some interviewers and our rating of policy, structures and resources, there was very little consistent implementation, and as the new ministry was in the process of capacitating itself, and in collaboration with considerable international networks, political change disestablished the ministry, separating higher education from science and technology, and relocating higher education with education. For some stakeholders, this separation of higher education from the science and technology portfolio was both a signal that the current government did not fully grasp the value of higher education for development, and that higher education was no longer a priority for the new Ministry of Education.

The above shows a very interesting progression and regression associated – as is so often the case in Africa – with regime change. The interpenetration of small elites means that there were not adequate boundaries between different spheres of the state; in other words, when there was a change in political leadership, it directly effected changes in the leadership of institutions such as the university. This is in contrast to more stable democracies with larger elites, such as the United Kingdom, where the change from labour party rule to a liberal/conservative coalition had no direct effect on the choice of the leadership at Oxford University.

In Mozambique it seemed that at the very moment that both government and the Eduardo Mondlane University leadership were moving towards the beginnings of a pact about the importance of high-level skills and knowledge production as a key component of development, a change of leadership and direction occurred. The new direction could be described as an attempt at massification, associated with the knowledge economy. This form of massification believes that broadening access, particularly through differentiation, even if of low quality, lifts the skills base and improves equity. It also brings credits to government for providing greater access to higher education, which is quite rightly seen as improving equity.

However, differentiation associated with globalisation and knowledge economies encourages both high-end research and innovation universities, along with a range of institutions that produce different levels and types of skills (e.g. the US spectrum from Harvard, to state land grant universities, to community colleges). The Mozambique example seemed to be going in another direction, that is, where higher education was important for social mobility and votes. So, while there seemed to be a pact that higher education is important for development, there was considerable disagreement on what a system of higher education that would contribute to development should look like.

What were some of the factors impacting on the university's capacity to contribute to development?

The first factor that impacts on the capacity of the university to make a contribution to development is the lack of a pact, or the changing pact. It appeared that from the late 1990s to the middle of the 2000s there was an attempt to move on the agenda towards a vision that knowledge, particularly science and technology, was important for development.

There was some considerable correspondence between government, the reorganisation of ministries, cooperation from the leadership of the institution, and the beginnings of funder coordination.

The *Strategic Plan for Higher Education in Mozambique (2000–2010)*, developed through an extensive consultative process involving major stakeholders and all provinces, was completed in August 2000. This was followed by the establishment of the Ministry of Higher Education, Science and Technology which led the last phase of the conception of the Strategic Plan, and which emerged as an important driving force in the process of working out the Operational Plan approved by the Cabinet and major funders such as World Bank and SIDA. This did not mean that academics had necessarily bought into this new direction, but at least at the national and institutional leadership levels there seemed to have been considerable movement towards a pact.

In other words, a number of conditions for the Eduardo Mondlane University to make a stronger contribution to development had been falling into place, and then it changed. The 2004 presidential and parliamentary election brought about a change in leadership in the country, ministry and the leadership of the university. The new direction of massive expansion, public and private, represented a different notion of the role of the university and, at the time of the study, there seemed to be considerable contestations within the institution.

Within the university the key factors that seemed to be weakening the academic core were poor graduation rates in its SET and other programmes, a low proportion of postgraduate students, accompanied by low numbers of doctoral students, and low output of research publications. This meant that the institution had not been gearing up, with the necessary policies and resource allocations, to fulfil the notion of a stronger knowledge contribution to development. A positive development was that the university was beginning to build up its student numbers in masters programmes.

A positive towards strengthening connectivity and knowledge was the greater coordination and institutionalisation of donor funding. Both the establishment of the Donor Coordination Unit and the number of development projects that strengthen the academic core, were examples of positive attempts to strengthen, and make development projects more sustainable. The fact that the university still has such small numbers of doctorates and low publication rates could be attributed to a number of reasons, such as that the institution started from a relatively low base and that it takes time to build knowledge capacity.

Finally, the absence of a pact meant that there was not a coordinated triangle of government, donors and the university. Universities and donor agencies cannot contribute meaningfully and sustainably to development alone; neither can donors play the role of a surrogate state because they do not have the resources for a sustainable economy of scale contribution.

10

South Africa and the Nelson Mandela Metropolitan University

10.1 The higher education and economic development context in South Africa

How did South Africa fare in meeting the 'preconditions' for an effective and productive relationship between higher education and economic development identified by Pillay's (2010b) investigation of three successful systems?

High-quality schooling: Participation rates were relatively high at both the primary and secondary levels. The net enrolment ratio in primary education was at 88% in 2006 but still left the country a bit short of achieving universal primary education (UNESCO 2009). The net enrolment ratio in secondary schooling was at around 65% in 2006, leaving considerable room for improvement.

However, quality of schooling remained the biggest challenge. An indication of the quality of schooling in South African education could be gained by an analysis of the Southern and Eastern Africa Consortium for Monitoring Educational Quality (SACMEQ) reading and mathematics scores. In SACMEQ II, conducted in 2005, South Africa came eighth out of 14 Southern and East African countries (after Botswana, Kenya, Mauritius, Mozambique, Seychelles, Swaziland and Tanzania) and ninth in mathematics (after the same seven countries listed earlier plus Uganda).

Inequality in South African society was also mirrored in the education outcomes by socio-economic status and region. Amongst the countries participating in SACMEQ II, with only one exception (mathematics in Lesotho), pupils from high socio-economic status backgrounds outscored pupils from low socio-economic status backgrounds in every country. What was of additional concern was the magnitude of the difference in the score in many countries.

On the reading scores, the difference between high and low socio-economic status students ranged from five points to 103. South Africa was the worst offender in this regard with the 103 point difference. On the mathematics scores, the difference ranged from -4 to 78, with South Africa again the worst offender.

Effective economic and education planning: A serious commitment to economic and education planning was reflected in the policy documents. However, there was little evidence that such planning was actually taking place. The policies were in place, as were the necessary institutions, but there was little evidence of effective planning between the economic and education/higher education sectors.

The role of the state: The state was playing an important role with respect to funding. The state's policy documents gave prominence to the role of tertiary education in development broadly, and in the further development of the knowledge economy in particular.

Partnerships: In general, no evidence could be gleaned of partnerships between the state, the universities and the private sector.

Institutional differentiation: Theoretically, universities were differentiated. In practice, however, they all appeared to aspire to the same goals with regard to teaching and research. At another level, the tertiary sector needs to be expanded to provide for a much broader role for colleges.

Quality: Serious questions had been raised about the quality of educational provision across the system. In the higher education sector, pockets of excellence coexisted with a number of poor-quality institutions. The finding on poor quality features prominently in the WEF's Global Competitiveness Index and the Global Innovation Index.

Funding: State funding of tertiary education was relatively high in African terms but, given the extent of need and the imperative to increase access and enhance equity, much more funding was needed. In addition, while the overall budget had increased over the past decade, the government subsidy per student had declined.

Innovation: In the African context, South Africa was performing very well in terms of international innovation indicators. However, this was because of a small, highly developed component of the society that was able to participate fully in the knowledge economy. The need for South Africa to broaden access and to improve equity and quality to ensure greater expansion of the knowledge economy segments was paramount.

10.2   Evidence of a pact around the role of higher education in South Africa?

South Africa's indicator ratings for the role of knowledge and universities in national and institutional policies and plans are presented in Table 35.

TABLE 35 Role for knowledge and universities in development in South Africa

National rating = 4/6			
The concept of a knowledge economy features in the national development plan	3 Strong Appears in a number of policies	**2 Weak** Only mentioned in one policy	1 Absent Not mentioned at all
A role for higher education in development in national policies and plans	3 Prevalent Clearly mentioned in development policies	**2 Weak**	1 Absent
University rating = 3/6			
Concept of a knowledge economy features in institutional policies and plans	3 Features strongly in strategic plan and/or research policy/ strategy	**2** Vague reference in strategic plan or research policy	1 Not mentioned at all
Institutional policies with regard to the university's role in economic development	3 Institutional policy	2 Embedded in strategic plan, research policy, etc.	**1** No formal policies

FINDINGS

- There was a lack of clarity and agreement (pact) about a development model and the role of higher education in development, at both national and institutional levels.
- South Africa, with its historical dependency on mineral extraction and thus a resource economy, had not accepted that knowledge, and by implication higher education, is key to development.
- The formation of a 'super ministry', which combined universities and training, was unprecedented in the context of the knowledge economy. It signalled that the government saw the universities from the traditional African post-liberation perspective of training professionals and for upward mobility (new elite formation).
- There was an emerging awareness about the importance of the knowledge economy approach, particularly in the Department of Science and Technology, but not in the Department of Education. Within the NMMU, it was surprisingly absent, except for specific pockets, mainly in the sciences.

Notions of the role of knowledge and universities in development

Table 36 summarises the notions of the role of higher education held by national and institutional stakeholders, and indicates whether the notion was strong, prevalent, present or absent altogether.

At the national level in South Africa, the notion of the role of the university varied – from training for the labour market and training researchers (Department of Higher Education and Training), to a strong emphasis on research and innovation (Department of Science and Technology), to skills and innovation policies aligned to sectoral priorities from the Cabinet's Industrial Policy Action Plan. These different government positions basically covered all four notions of the role of knowledge and universities in development. A senior university leader argued that the Mbeki administration did not see higher education as central to debates on macro-economic development and that it was only towards the end of his administration that the issue was raised intermittently. Now, the Minister of Higher Education and Training was focussing on training for the labour market.

What was fascinating was that this lack of agreement about the role of higher education among the key government stakeholders was mirrored, and even amplified, within the NMMU. A university leader put it so eloquently that it is worth repeating here:

> Universities are at a crossing point with a number of contradictory tensions that are written into their very constitutional character. They're entrepreneurial and scholastic, on the one hand; on the other hand, they're conservative and then radical; they're traditional and they're forward-looking, and they have to serve long-term knowledge markets, the fundamental blue sky research imperatives, versus functional research that could make an impact; applied research in the here and now. They produce students that we hope will find work or be employable, yet they do not have control over what happens to those products once they generate them.

He concluded that there was no single, dominant view about the role of higher education in South Africa and that each university effectively made up its own rules.

The views of university respondents on the role of the NMMU in relation to development were very varied. One respondent reflected that current demands required political trade-offs which might result in a view of the university as a luxury at worst, or at best an institution that should deliver skills for the labour market. Other views included that the university's real contribution to development is broadening the researcher pool; that it is through technology development and transfer; and, that it lies in stimulating economic activity in the immediate vicinity of the university. There was also a view that linking the university to economic development was a recurring fad. Perhaps not surprisingly, much of the discussion in the interviews was about the ongoing internal debates about the identity of the newly-merged 'comprehensive' institution.

As can be seen from Table 36, overall at the NMMU, there was no dominant view; instead, there were a range of competing views representing all four notions. People from the previous university seemed to favour the self-governing and the engine view, while staff from the previous technikon leaned more towards an instrumental role. The ancillary notion also had some support, even though it was less strongly expressed. In conclusion, two things stood out: firstly, everybody was acutely aware of the debate about the identity of the 'comprehensive university' and its possible role with regards to development and, secondly, there was absolutely no agreement.

TABLE 36 Comparing national and institutional notions of the role of higher education in South Africa

Notions		National stakeholders		University stakeholders
Ancillary	⚬	Strongly present in some policy documents	☐	Some academics thought that this is how the university is perceived
Self-governing	■	Accepted in a number of policies and expected to provide general education and train researchers	☐	Very strong amongst some stakeholders
Instrument for development agendas	■	Probably most directly expressed by Cabinet document	☐	Many academic see the 'technikon' model as the future with technology application
Engine for development	☐	Very strongly favoured by the Department of Science and Technology	☐	Some academics see globally competitive research and innovation as the way to go

Key:

■ Strong   ☐ Present   ⚬ Absent

FINDINGS

- In terms of notions of the role of the university in development, at the national level there was an unresolved tension between the self-governance and instrumental roles. This reflected the well known tension between institutional autonomy, on the one hand, and engagement or responsiveness, on the other.
- At the institutional level, the merger between three institutions with different notions of the role of a higher education institution was evident in the lack of resolution amongst institutional stakeholders.
- At neither national nor institutional level was there agreement about the role of the university in development. It was quite surprising that amongst university leadership there was such low support for a knowledge economy approach.

10.3 The academic core of the Nelson Mandela Metropolitan University

The analysis of the university's academic core presented in the case study report was undertaken on the basis of the rating of seven key indicators as 'strong', 'medium' or 'weak'. The data on which the ratings are based are contained in the detailed case study report.[21] The seven indicators and their ratings are presented in Table 37.

TABLE 37 Nelson Mandela Metropolitan University: Rating of the academic core

Indicator		Rating (strong/medium/weak)*
1	Science, engineering and technology enrolments and graduations	SET students = 31% in 2007, and increasing. But only 60% of SET intakes expected to graduate
2	Postgraduate/undergraduate enrolments ratio Masters/PhD enrolment ratio	Proportion of postgraduates low at 11% in 2001 and in 2007. However, masters and doctors enrolments grew and ratio between masters and doctoral enrolments satisfactory at 6:1
3	Teaching load: Academic staff–student ratio	Overall ratio 28:1 in 2007, and 23: 1 in SET. Both unsatisfactory
4	Proportion of academic staff with doctorates	34% of permanent academics have doctorates, which is the South African average
5	Research income per permanent academic staff member**	Moderate at PPP$ 12 300
6	Doctoral graduates	Graduates on average from 2001 to 2007 constituted 5.5% of permanent academics
7	Research publications	Outputs in 2007 about 60% of targets set for research universities

Key:

■ Strong   ■ Medium   □ Weak

* Refer to Appendix F for a detailed descriptions of the academic core rating categories.

** The research income data are based on figures in the official university 2007 income statements.

The following observations can be made about the academic core data for NMMU:

1. **SET enrolments**: The university's SET enrolments grew from 5 900 in 2001 to 7 400 in 2007, at an average annual rate of 3.7%. Because of the sharp drop that occurred in its teacher education enrolments, NMMU's proportion of SET students rose from 18% in 2001 to 31% in 2007. Its SET graduation rate, however, declined over the period. Only about 60% of students entering SET programmes in NMMU were likely to complete their qualifications.

2. **Postgraduate enrolments**: The proportion of postgraduate students in the university's total enrolment was 11% in both 2001 and 2007. Masters enrolments did, however, grow from 1 100 in 2001 to 1 332 in 2007, at an average annual increase of 3.2%. The masters graduation rate was below the target set for South African universities but was satisfactory. Doctoral enrolments doubled from 175 in 2001 to 327 in 2007. Doctoral enrolments had, in 2007, a share of 20% of the masters plus doctoral total. This implies that there should be a flow of masters graduates into doctoral studies.

---

21   The South Africa and Nelson Mandela Metropolitan University case study report is available at www.chet.org.za.

3. **Teaching load**: Between 2001 and 2007, NMMU's FTE academic staff total grew at double the annual growth rate in FTE students. Its average FTE student to FTE academic staff ratio, as a consequence, fell from 31:1 in 2001 to 28:1 in 2007. NMMU's SET ratio was 23:1 in 2007, which was high by South African standards. NMMU's permanent academics appeared to have heavy teaching loads which may make it difficult for them to engage in research activities.

4. **Qualifications of staff**: In 2007, 34% of NMMU's permanent academic staff had doctorates as their highest formal qualifications. This was close to the average for South African universities, but was below the proportions reported by research-intensive universities.

5. **Research funding**: NMMU had, in 2007, PPP$ 12 300 (or USD 7 600) in research funding per permanent academic staff member. This was a reasonable amount, but was below the sums available to South Africa's research-intensive universities.

6. **Doctoral graduates**: Graduates increased from 27 in 2001 to 35 in 2007, which was a very modest increase of 4.4%. This did not reflect the considerable increase in doctoral enrolments, from 175 in 2001 to 327 in 2007, which was almost a 50% growth. Neither was this strong growth reflected in outputs, and was quite surprising given that masters enrolments only increased from 1 100 to 1 332 (8%) over the same period.

7. **Research publications**: In terms of research publications, NMMU's output was moderate. Its 2007 ratio of publication units per permanent academic was, at 0.34, below the ratio of 0.50 which had been set as a target for South Africa's research universities.

In terms of the previous discussion about the four competing notions of the role of the university amongst institutional stakeholders at NMMU, the academic core data told a different story. Firstly, the institution was changing dramatically from a predominantly undergraduate social sciences/humanities (67% in 2001) to a SET (31%) and business management (25%) institution, with the social sciences/humanities declining to 24%. Secondly, the proportion of postgraduate enrolment was very small – not much better than the University of Ghana – and neither the postgraduate enrolments nor the doctoral graduates had increased by much (NMMU went from 27 doctoral graduates in 2001 to 35 in 2007). Thirdly, NMMU had the poorest student–staff ratio of the institutions compared, while the percentage of staff with doctorates was also the lowest. Fourthly, research income was a fraction of that of research-intensive universities in South Africa. Doctoral output had remained stagnant, despite an almost doubling of enrolments. The 5.5% doctoral graduates per permanent academic staff member were well below the target of 10%. And, finally, the research output was only 0.34, slightly up from 0.30 in 2001, but well below the modest government target of 0.50.

NMMU was, therefore, really an undergraduate teaching institution, with a strong shift towards SET and business management. This implied a strong instrumental orientation, while the institution's knowledge-producing capacity (increasing proportion of doctorates amongst staff and students and an increase in publications) did not position it to be a strong self-governing institution, nor an engine of development.

FINDINGS

- The knowledge production output variables of the academic core did not seem strong enough to enable NMMU to make a sustained contribution to development.
- The university was not significantly changing from a predominantly undergraduate teaching institution. However, it was changing from a mainly undergraduate social science/humanities to more of a SET and business studies institution. In that sense it was moving closer to a number of other African universities such as Nairobi and Mauritius.
- On the input side, NMMU scored medium in comparison with the rest of the sample with regards to postgraduate enrolments, student–staff ratios, staff with doctorates and research income.
- On the output side, NMMU scored medium both with regards to doctoral graduates and research outputs, but both were very low in comparison to an institution such as the University of Cape Town.
- The most serious challenges to strengthening the academic core seemed to be around increasing the percentage of staff with doctorates, doctoral graduation rates and research outputs.

10.4 Coordination and connectedness

Knowledge policy coordination and implementation

Table 38 presents the ratings for the coordination of knowledge policies at the national level. As was highlighted earlier, South Africa had produced a plethora of policy documents in all sectors, but especially in economic development and education. In addition, institutional structures and mechanisms had been developed for coordination of policy. These included clusters of departments at the national level (e.g. for the economic and social sectors), MinMecs (Minister plus provincial Members of the Executive Council for a particular sector), and budget structures that included all three spheres. And, the Medium Term Strategic Framework was a very important document that identified priorities and defined cross-cutting policies that needed to achieve the medium-term objectives as well as the role of government.

However, the biggest challenge that faced government was the coordination and effective implementation of policies. For example, it did not seem that any collaboration was taking place between the Department of Higher Education and Training (DHET) and the Department of Science and Technology (DST) to ensure progress on their respective roles around the enhancement of knowledge production. And, while the DST had world-class research and innovation policies, the DHET had not even developed a plan for research, as was promised in the 1997 White Paper. Instead, the orientation of the DHET was towards linking higher education and the labour market, as reflected in the creation of a Ministry of Higher Education and Training, while in other parts of Africa (e.g. Kenya and Mauritius) and in many other countries in the world, higher education was integrated with science and technology.

A senior academic at the NMMU asserted that not only was the claim that the Department of Education supported development 'a figment of somebody's imagination', but that the Department and the National Research Foundation's funding policies could be considered 'anti-development'. For instance, the Department had stopped funding patents and the Foundation only supported small-scale individual projects, thereby encouraging projectisation rather than large-scale development projects or programmes.

If there was not much direction from the national Department of Education, then provincial governments certainly did not provide much input either. In part this was because many of them were quite weak, like in the Eastern Cape, and were battling just to hold themselves together, and there was considerable political instability amongst the senior leadership. In addition, universities were often seen as either esoteric spaces or simply as a national (and not provincial) competency.

TABLE 38 National coordination of knowledge policies in South Africa

National rating = 6/9			
Economic development and higher education planning are linked	3 Systematic Formal structures Headed by senior minister	**2 Sporadic** Clusters/forums	1 Weak Occasional meetings
Link between universities and national authorities	3 Specific coordination structures or agencies	**2** Some formal structures but no meaningful coordination	1 No structures, and political rather than professional networks
Coordination and consensus building of government agencies involved in higher education	3 Higher education mainstreamed across government departments	**2** Intermittent interaction with ineffective forums	1 Higher education issues limited mainly to one ministry or directorate

FINDINGS

- At the national level, there were considerable coordination activities, including clusters and the reorganisation of the national education ministry. However, there seemed to be no improvement in the historical non-coordination between different ministries, particularly higher education and science and technology.
- While there may have been some personal networks between government officials and some university leaders, these did not seem to contribute towards strengthening the sector as they tended to be more orientated towards political rather than productive advantage – a widespread problem in Africa.
- As is the case in the other seven countries, South Africa had a tertiary or higher education council which could help strengthen national governance capacity, but it was undergoing 'role redefinition'.

Table 39 summarises the ratings of the indicators relating to the implementation of knowledge policies and activities at both the national and university levels.

TABLE 39 Implementation of knowledge policies and activities in South Africa

National rating = 11/12			
Role of the ministry responsible for higher education	3 Organised ministry with capacity to make predictable allocations	**2** Spots of capacity with some steering instruments	1 Weak capacity with unpredictable allocations
Implementation to 'steer' higher education towards development	**3 Strong** Instruments such as funding/ special projects that incentivise institutions/individuals	2 Weak Occasional grants for special projects	1 Absent No particular incentive funding
Balance/ratio of sources of income for institutions	**3** Government, fees and third stream	2 Mainly government plus student fees	1 Mainly government with external funders
Funding consistency	**3** A stable, transparent public funding mechanism based on criteria agreed upon by all actors involved	2 Funding allocations somewhat predictable but do not allow for long-term planning nor reward enterprising behaviour	1 No clear funding or incentives from government
University rating = 13/18			
Specific units, funding or appointments linked to economic development	3 Specific units, funding or appointments	2 Economic development initiatives aspect of a unit or appointment	**1** Mainly ad hoc, staff-initiated operations
Incentives and rewards for development-related activities	3 Incentives/counts towards promotion	**2** Some signals but largely rhetoric	1 No mention
Teaching programmes linked to the labour market	**3** Targets for enrolments in fields considered to be of high economic relevance	2 Some programmes in response to specific industry requests	1 No new programmes linked to labour market
Special programmes linking students to economic development	3 Entrepreneurship, work-based learning and/or incubators for students mainstreamed	**2** Ad hoc programmes	1 No special programmes
Research activities becoming more economy-oriented	3 Research policy/strategy has an economic development focus	**2** Some research agendas have an economic development focus	1 Ad hoc project funding
Levels of government and institutional funding for research	**3** High	2 Medium	1 Low

FINDINGS

- At the national level, one of the weaknesses was implementation: while South Africa did have steering instruments and mechanisms, there was no national human resource plan in the context of a development approach/model.
- While NMMU did have development-related structures and special programmes linking the university to development initiatives, the problem was that in too many cases these initiatives were driven by individuals rather than being institutionalised. In addition, these special implementation efforts need to be more connected.
- Despite policies that extol the importance of research related to development activities (mainly through focus themes), research related to development was not rewarded through incentives beyond the traditional academic promotion system.

The NMMU's connectedness to external stakeholders and the academic core

Much of what could be considered the NMMU's 'development-related activities' would fall under the engagement mandate. However, what exactly constituted 'engagement' was being debated as energetically as the identity of the university, and of course these two issues were related. In addition, while there were incentives for staff to engage in innovation, there were no such incentives for other kinds of engagement activities, and community engagement was seen as the 'black sheep' in terms of funding support.

Although there was no formal coordination of linkages with business and industry, these linkages appeared to be strong at the level of individual units, departments and some faculties, as was demonstrated by the development-related projects/centres included in the study and highlighted in the institution's 2008 Self-Evaluation Report. However, a university leader asserted that while the institution had a relationship with a few specific companies, in general there were very few university–industry partnerships or relationships at the institutional level.

So again, not unlike at the national level, there seemed to be a wide range of activities and a large number of projects, but these were mostly uncoordinated and taking place without any real clarity of how they fit into the university's as yet undefined role in development.

With regard to the connectedness of development-related activities to the academic core, the articulation and academic ratings applied to the six projects/centres are presented in Figure 9.

FIGURE 9 **Plotting the development-related projects/centres at the Nelson Mandela Metropolitan University**

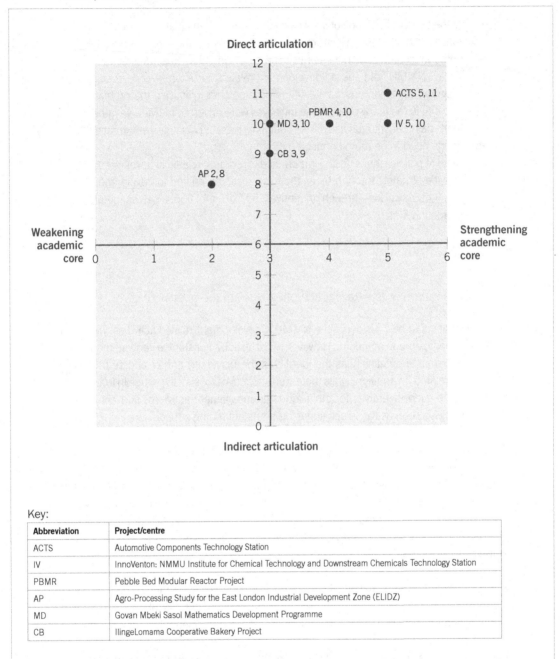

Key:

Abbreviation	Project/centre
ACTS	Automotive Components Technology Station
IV	InnoVenton: NMMU Institute for Chemical Technology and Downstream Chemicals Technology Station
PBMR	Pebble Bed Modular Reactor Project
AP	Agro-Processing Study for the East London Industrial Development Zone (ELIDZ)
MD	Govan Mbeki Sasol Mathematics Development Programme
CB	IlingeLomama Cooperative Bakery Project

FINDINGS

- While there was evidence of connectedness between the university and industry or the private sector, this was generally confined to the level of units or centres rather than institutional-level partnerships.
- Unlike most of the universities in the study (except for Mauritius), the NMMU was involved in a wide array of R&D consultancies with, or for, industry.
- Projects/centres that were considered by university leadership to be strongly connected to development tended to score well on the articulation indicators – in other words, they reflected national priorities (and to a lesser extent institutional objectives), had more than one funding source and, in some cases, plans for financial sustainability, and may have had a connection to an implementation agency.
- A number of these projects/centres also managed to keep a strong connection to the academic core of the university, whilst some were more disconnected from these core knowledge activities.
- There were 'exemplary' development projects/centres. The problem was scale: there were simply not enough, and some seemed overly dependent on exceptional individuals.

10.5 Concluding comments about the South Africa/NMMU case study

In the African context, South Africa was performing very well in terms of international innovation indicators. In our sample, only Mauritius outscored it on the World Bank knowledge economy index, except for innovation, good scientific research institutions (South African ranked 29th in the world), and collaboration between universities and business in the area of innovation. South Africa thus had in place a very strong 'architecture' for research and innovation, albeit a very small sector in which only a select, highly-developed component of the society was able to participate. (Mauritius far outperformed South Africa in the HDI rating and equity.)

At the national level, a very complex picture emerged. There were seven major policy documents – starting with the famous Reconstruction and Development Programme – all dealing with development and, to a greater or lesser extent, with human capital development (improving schooling, special skills, work-based training, etc.). However, none of these dealt strongly with a knowledge economy as driver for the economy. The Human Resource Development Strategy (2009) listed as the last three of 15 strategic priorities that South Africa must be ranked in the top 10% of comparable countries in terms of knowledge and human capital stock. The real global-orientated research, innovation and human resource development for science and technology comes from the Department of Science and

Technology which says that South Africa has to shift from a resource-based economy to a knowledge economy. In this regard, the four interconnected pillars were innovation, economic and institutional infrastructure, information technology, and education. This information was drawn directly from the World Bank knowledge economy index.

However, as was illustrated above, despite structures and mechanisms between government departments, and between government and universities, to ensure coordination and implementation, this was not happening. Coordination of policies require agreement on the role of knowledge, and higher education, in development. And in South Africa there was neither. As the highly successful soccer world cup showed, resources and capacity were not as big a constraint as in the rest of the continent. For once in the 'new' South Africa there was agreement on a goal and a wide diversity of resources were mobilised to achieve this goal – along with strict intentional monitoring of progress.

However, with regards to higher education there were competing notions without a pact as to how to resolve it. Different policies, and a range of interviews, revealed widely divergent notions of the role of the university in development. Some respondents even questioned whether the university had more than an ancillary role to play. The absence of a pact emerged as a possible contributor to explaining the endemic lack of coordination and implementation outlined above.

One major problem seemed to be that while there was broad agreement in the society about the importance of education, education was seen as a key mobility mechanism for individual enhancement. This was part of the enormous emphasis on equity which meant that education was essentially for social mobility and the promotion of equality. Sadly, as all the statistics show, the South African education system (post-secondary, in particular) had not yet delivered on this promise, except for a rather small minority.

What were some of the factors impacting on the university's capacity to contribute to development?

In terms of input variables, NMMU had teaching loads which probably made it difficult for academic staff to engage in research activities. A further problem was that the proportion of postgraduate students at NMMU remained low, even though masters and doctoral student enrolments had increased. Another issue was that the proportion of academic staff with doctorates was below that normally found in a research-intensive university. In terms of output variables, such as the production of research publications and the weighted output of publications plus research graduates, NMMU's performance was below the targets set for South African universities. The key factors that seemed to be weakening NMMU's academic core were (a) the low proportions of postgraduate students, (b) the high student to academic staff ratios (particularly in SET), (c) the moderate outputs of graduates in research degrees, and (d) the low publication output rate relative to the targets set for South African universities. A positive development was that NMMU was experiencing a growth in masters and doctoral enrolments, which should begin to provide an underpinning for research programmes.

A related problem was that the university was 'conflicted' by its contested identity, meaning that it would be difficult to allocate resources to strengthen the academic core. This was partially reflected in the assessment of development-related projects and centres. Two of the centres engaged in a large number and variety of consultancy projects for industry, which in part explains their strong articulation/connectedness rating. What was also interesting about these two projects was that despite the strong orientation towards consultancy, they also managed to make significant contributions to strengthening the academic core of the university.

That the short-term consultancy project, as well as the two characterised more as 'community service' type activities, scored quite highly on the articulation/connectedness rating was perhaps not surprising. However, these types of projects weaken the academic core by drawing academic staff away from their core functions. While it could be argued that the projects which are weakening the academic core were making a contribution to development in terms of an instrumentalist notion of the university, in terms of our analytical framework, this is not a sustainable position that will enhance the longer-term contribution of the university.

In conclusion, why not revisit Burton Clark (1983), since 2011 was the year that the Consortium of Higher Education Researchers (CHER) conference honoured him with a memorial keynote session. Almost 20 years ago, Clark (1983: 193–194) had the following to say about 'comprehensive' universities:

> The modern comprehensive university in some countries represents an effort to have it both ways, to allow for differentiation of major parts and, at the same time, assign formal equality that hopefully will keep down individual distinctions. But this form appears unstable, especially in large systems, as the more prestigious parts resist the lumping together of everyone and as attentive publics as well as insiders perceive real differences and attach different values to the parts. … As those in the Italian system have been painfully finding out, the nationalized public university alone cannot zigzag in all the many directions called for by an increasing heterogeneity of function. It does not adapt well to new types of students, new connections to labour markets, or new academic fields, especially when they viewed to be of lower status. … [T]he university, becomes overloaded and risks a loss of concentration of resources and attention upon its traditional activities. Everyone then feels caught in a difficult situation, leading to a sense of continuing crisis.

11
Tanzania and the
University of Dar es Salaam

11.1 The higher education and economic development context in Tanzania

How did Tanzania fare in meeting the 'preconditions' for an effective and productive relationship between higher education and economic development identified by Pillay's (2010b) investigation of three successful systems?

High-quality schooling: Although statistics were not available, anecdotal evidence suggested that the participation rate at the secondary level was extremely low. Access and equity (in terms of gender) at the primary level had reached commendable levels. However, the proportion of the primary school-leaving cohort that was able to enter secondary schooling was extremely low, mainly because of low levels of public investment. There was evidence that the primary education system was relatively efficient. Repetition rates were low and the survival rate to the last grade of primary schooling was 83% in 2006 (the average for sub-Saharan Africa was 67% and that for developing countries, 81%) (UNESCO 2009).

Effective economic and education planning: There was no official commitment to economic and education planning, although the link between economic development and education, especially tertiary education, was recognised. For example, the *Tanzania Development Vision 2025* recognised the role of tertiary education in developing the critical human resources necessary for development.

The role of the state: The state was playing an important role with respect to funding, as well as encouraging private sector provision of higher education. In fact, state funding was relatively high compared to other countries in the region. However, the state was dependent on donor funding for a significant part of its budget, including that of higher education.

Partnerships: In general, no evidence could be obtained of partnerships between the state, the universities and the private sector.

Institutional differentiation: There was little evidence of differentiation amongst universities.

Quality: The WEF was highly critical of quality in the Tanzanian education system. However, the country had performed relatively well in regional tests of proficiency of primary children in reading and mathematics. In the 2005 SACMEQ assessment, Tanzania was outperformed in reading only by Kenya and the Seychelles amongst East and Southern African countries, and in mathematics by Kenya, Mauritius, Mozambique and Seychelles. It would appear that Tanzania had developed a relatively successful (in terms of access and quality) primary education system but had not been able to expand quantitatively or qualitatively beyond this level.

Funding: State funding of tertiary education was relatively high in regional terms but it was not clear whether outputs and outcomes were commensurate with the levels of investment.

Innovation: At the time of the study, Tanzania had not invested sufficiently either in its universities or its private sector in terms of research and innovation. R&D investment approximated only about 0.2% of GDP, well below the developing country benchmark of 1%.

11.2   Evidence of a pact around the role of higher education in Tanzania?

Tanzania's indicator ratings for the role of knowledge and universities in national and institutional policies and plans are presented in Table 40.

At the national level, Tanzania was increasingly aware of putting a higher premium on human capacity development. In the 'Developmental Mindset and Empowering Culture' goal in *Vision 2025*, key factors included a broad human development strategy, a learning society, and education as strategic change agent. This was reflected in the somewhat positive ratings for the concept of a knowledge economy featuring in the national development plan, and a role for higher education in development in national policies and plans. However, in the *Vision 2025* four obstacles to achieving this were mentioned, including donor dependency, low capacity for economic management, failures of good government, and 'ineffective implementation syndrome'. These problems were reflected in the weak ratings about spots of capacity in the department of education and unsystematic steering. In summary, at the national level there was certainly an increasing awareness of the importance of the knowledge economy, but policies, resources and incentives were not allocated accordingly. In addition, the higher education system was not sufficiently differentiated, and with a very low participation rate.

At the University of Dar es Salaam, there was a strong narrative amongst institutional stakeholders about the role of the university in development. However, this role had not yet been clarified, nor was it strongly reflected in institutional policies or structures (mainly ad hoc staff initiatives). The notion of the knowledge economy was rather absent in university leadership discourses, but there was a more concentrated attempt to link research to economic development. In terms of linking teaching programmes to the labour market there was considerable emphasis on entrepreneurship, but there were not systematic, university-wide linkages to business. There was a strong influence of the Millennium Development Goals, driven by development aid, and these activities were increasingly better institutionalised.

TABLE 40 Role for knowledge and universities in development in Tanzania

National rating = 5/6			
The concept of a knowledge economy features in the national development plan	3 Strong Appears in a number of policies	**2 Weak** Only mentioned in one policy	1 Absent Not mentioned at all
A role for higher education in development in national policies and plans	**3 Prevalent** Clearly mentioned in development policies	2 Weak	1 Absent
University rating = 3/6			
Concept of a knowledge economy features in institutional policies and plans	3 Features strongly in strategic plan and/or research policy/ strategy	**2** Vague reference in strategic plan or research policy	1 Not mentioned at all
Institutional policies with regard to the university's role in economic development	3 Institutional policy	2 Embedded in strategic plan, research policy, etc.	**1** No formal policies

FINDINGS

- At the national level, the importance of the knowledge economy was weak, but the importance of higher education was strongly reflected in national policy statements.
- In contrast, at the institutional level, there was only vague reference to the knowledge economy and no formal policies regarding the university's role in development.
- There was no broad agreement that knowledge, and by implication higher education, is key to development.

Notions of the role of knowledge and universities in development

Table 41 summarises the notions of the role of higher education held by national and institutional stakeholders, and indicates whether the notion was strong, prevalent, present or absent altogether.

TABLE 41 Comparing national and institutional notions of the role of higher education in Tanzania

Notions		National stakeholders		University stakeholders
Ancillary	■	Ambiguity about being an ancillary and an instrument	☐	Trying to move away from this position
Self-governing	•	No obvious tensions	☐	Some staff still support indirect contribution to development
Instrument for development agendas	■	Strong opinions about not enough application of expertise of staff for development	■	Strong awareness linked to consultancy and donor projectssome staff
Engine for development	☐	Mentioned in some planning documents	•	A discourse developing but not reflected in policies

Key:

■ Strong ☐ Present • Absent

FINDINGS

- In terms of notions of the role of the university in development, at the national level there was considerable ambiguity about the role of the university – being an ancillary and needing to be an instrument of development.
- At the institutional level, there was a strong leaning towards an instrument for development notion, but a very weak discourse about the engine of development notion.
- At neither national nor institutional levels was there agreement about the role of the university in development. It was quite surprising that amongst university leadership there was such low support for a knowledge economy approach.

11.3 The academic core of the University of Dar es Salaam

The analysis of the university's academic core presented in the case study report was undertaken on the basis of the rating of seven key indicators as 'strong', 'medium' or 'weak'. The data on which the ratings are based are contained in the detailed case study report.[22] The seven indicators and their ratings are presented in Table 42.

---

22   The Tanzania and University of Dar es Salaam case study report is available at www.chet.org.za.

TABLE 42 **University of Dar es Salaam: Rating of the academic core**

Indicator		Rating (strong/medium/weak)*
1	Science, engineering and technology enrolments and graduations	Proportion of SET enrolments = 36%. Graduate output rate good
2	Postgraduate/undergraduate enrolments ratio Masters/PhD enrolment ratio	Proportion of postgraduates in enrolment increased to 15% in 2007. But proportion of doctoral enrolments remained low
3	Teaching load: Academic staff–student ratio	Overall ratio of 14:1 in 2007
4	Proportion of academic staff with doctorates	50% with doctorates
5	Research income per permanent academic staff member**	Low at PPP$ 6 400
6	Doctoral graduates	Graduates in 2007 constituted 2.18% of permanent academics
7	Research publications	Output of publications per academic (0.08) plus research graduates only 33% of target rate

Key:

■ Strong   ▩ Medium   ☐ Weak

* Refer to Appendix F for a detailed descriptions of the academic core rating categories.

** No specific information provided on research funding. All donor funding assumed to be research income.

The following observations can be made about the academic core data for the University of Dar es Salaam:

1. **SET enrolments:** The university's SET enrolments grew from 4 200 in 2001 to 6 600 in 2007. The average annual SET growth rate was 7.8% over this period, which was only half the growth rate of total enrolments. The proportion of SET students as a consequence dropped from 52% in 2001 to 36% in 2007. The university's SET graduation rate, however, improved over this period.

2. **Postgraduate enrolments:** The university's proportion of postgraduate students in its total enrolment grew from 9% in 2001 to 15% in 2007. This resulted from a rapid increase in masters enrolments, which grew from 552 in 2007 to 2 165 in 2007. The masters graduates total did not increase at the same rate as the enrolment total. The masters graduation rate remained, however, satisfactory. Doctoral enrolments increased from 54 in 2001 to 190 in 2007, but still had a share of only 8% of the masters plus doctors total. This implied that the flow of masters graduates into doctoral studies may not have been high enough to sustain strong research activities. Doctoral graduation rates furthermore remained low over the period.

3. **Teaching load:** Between 2001 and 2007, the university's FTE academic staff total grew at average annual growth rate below that of the rate of growth in FTE students. Its FTE student to FTE academic staff ratio was nevertheless a favourable one, rising from 11:1 in 2001 to 14:1 in 2007. The university's permanent academics must, in 2007, have had teaching loads which should have enabled them to engage in research activities, including the supervision of research students.

4. **Qualifications of staff**: In 2007, 50% of the university's permanent academic staff had doctorates as their highest formal qualifications. This was a proportion which matched those of South African universities which were strong in research.
5. **Research funding**: The estimates calculated suggest that the university research funding might not have been sufficient to sustain strong research activities.
6. **Doctoral graduates**: Doctoral graduates increased from 10 in 2001 to 20 in 2007, which was a doubling, but from a very low base. A very positive development was that doctoral enrolments tripled over the same period. The rather low ratio of 2.18% of doctoral graduates to permanent academic staff meant that the university could not reproduce itself.
7. **Research outputs**: In terms of research publications, the university's output was low. Its 2007 ratio of publication units per permanent academic was, at 0.08, well below the ratio of 0.50 which had been set as a target for South Africa's research universities.

In terms of input variables, the university had teaching loads which should have enabled its academic staff to support research activities. It also had a high proportion of academic staff with doctorates. In terms of output variables such as the production of research publications and of doctoral graduates, the university's performance was unsatisfactory. The key factors that seemed to be weakening the academic core were (a) the decline in the proportion of SET students, (b) the low proportions of masters and doctoral students, (c) the low numbers of students in the doctoral research stream, (d) the low output of doctoral graduates, (e) a shortage of research funding, and (e) the poor output of research publications. A positive development was that the university was experiencing a rapid growth in masters enrolments which could lead to growth in research programmes.

FINDINGS

- The knowledge production output variables of the academic core did not seem strong enough to enable the university to make a sustainable contribution to development.
- The university was not significantly changing from a predominantly undergraduate teaching institution.
- On the input side, the university scored strongly on three input variables (SET enrolments, staff teaching load and staff qualifications), but weak on the knowledge production indicators (doctoral graduation rates and research output).
- The most serious challenges to strengthening the academic core seemed to be to translate input strengths to output productivity.

11.4   Coordination and connectedness

Knowledge policy coordination and implementation

Table 43 presents the ratings for the coordination of knowledge policies at the national level. There were limited formal linkages or coordination between the different stakeholders in the pact. Specifically, there was no real linkage between economic development and higher education planning at the ministerial level, and higher education issues were limited to only one ministry. And, while there were some formal structures linking universities to national authorities, there was no meaningful coordination between the two. In summary, at the national level, the lack of policy linkages and coordination would make implementation very difficult to achieve.

TABLE 43 National coordination of knowledge policies in Tanzania

National rating = 4/9		
Economic development and higher education planning are linked	3 Systematic Formal structures Headed by senior minister	2 Sporadic Clusters/forums	**1 Weak** Occasional meetings
Link between universities and national authorities	3 Specific coordination structures or agencies	**2** Some formal structures but no meaningful coordination	1 No structures, and political rather than professional networks
Coordination and consensus building of government agencies involved in higher education	3 Higher education mainstreamed across government departments	2 Intermittent interaction with ineffective forums	**1** Higher education issues limited mainly to one ministry or directorate

FINDINGS

- At the national level, there seemed to be many informal interactions, but few institutionalised processes of coordination.
- While there were considerable personal networks between government officials and particular university leaders, it was not clear whether this was contributing towards strengthening the institution or the sector.

Table 44 summarises the ratings of the indicators relating to the implementation of knowledge policies and activities at both the national and university levels.

TABLE 44 Implementation of knowledge policies and activities in Tanzania

National rating = 7/12			
Role of the ministry responsible for higher education	3 Organised ministry with capacity to make predictable allocations	**2** Spots of capacity with some steering instruments	1 Weak capacity with unpredictable allocations
Implementation to 'steer' higher education towards development	3 Strong Instruments such as funding/special projects that incentivise institutions/individuals	**2 Weak** Occasional grants for special projects	1 Absent No particular incentive funding
Balance/ratio of sources of income for institutions	3 Government, fees and third stream	2 Mainly government plus student fees	**1** Mainly government with external funders
Funding consistency	3 A stable, transparent public funding mechanism based on criteria agreed upon by all actors involved	**2** Funding allocations somewhat predictable but do not allow for long-term planning nor reward enterprising behaviour	1 No clear funding or incentives from government
University rating = 10/18			
Specific units, funding or appointments linked to economic development	3 Specific units, funding or appointments	2 Economic development initiatives aspect of a unit or appointment	**1** Mainly ad hoc, staff-initiated operations
Incentives and rewards for development-related activities	3 Incentives/counts towards promotion	2 Some signals but largely rhetoric	**1** No mention
Teaching programmes linked to the labour market	3 Targets for enrolments in fields considered to be of high economic relevance	**2** Some programmes in response to specific industry requests	1 No new programmes linked to labour market
Special programmes linking students to economic development	**3** Entrepreneurship, work-based learning and/or incubators for students mainstreamed	2 Ad hoc programmes	1 No special programmes
Research activities are becoming more economy-oriented	3 Research policy/strategy has an economic development focus	**2** Some research agendas have an economic development focus	1 Ad hoc project funding
Levels of government and institutional funding for research	3 High	2 Medium	**1** Low

FINDINGS

- At the national level, the Department of Education was beginning to develop some capacity and steering, but this clearly needed to be strengthened.
- At the institutional level, the University of Dar es Salaam had one of the biggest entrepreneurship work-based programmes in the sample of institutions. However, while the university did have development-related structures and special programmes linking it to development initiatives, the problem was that in too many cases these initiatives were driven by individuals rather than being institutionalised. Also, these special implementation efforts needed to be more connected.
- The university, within tight budget constraints, was trying to increase research related to development activities. However, research related to development was not significantly rewarded through incentives beyond the traditional academic promotion system.

The University of Dar es Salaam's connectedness to external stakeholders and the academic core

In the university's strategic plan (2009), a wide range of external stakeholders was listed – from parliamentarians to the general public. However, in interviews there was frequent mention of a lack of engagement, even in the formulation of the plan itself. In the plan it was also mentioned that the university had not done well in marketing its outputs. While it was noted that linkages with organisations outside of Tanzania had been strengthened, linkages with local government, private sector, non-governmental and community-based organisations were still weak.

The main form of engagement was through consultancy projects which, according to the strategic plan, had more than doubled over the past decade (although this was probably an under count, as was the trend in terms of consultancies worldwide). More than 60% of all consultancy projects were undertaken for foreign agencies and the strategic plan noted that the university had not been very successful in securing consultancies from the government or the public sector in general.

Foreign donors appeared to play a significant funding role in the university. While some donors did assert their own agendas in the funding relationship, it appeared that the Department of Planning and Finance was playing an important and effective role in managing the interaction between internal institutional interests and those of the development partners.

Apart from project-related linkages with donors, there were some direct links between specific academic units or institutes and government ministries, such as the College of Engineering and the ministries such as Infrastructure and Science and Technology, the

Institute of Resource Assessment and the Ministry of Agriculture, and the Economic Research Bureau with the Ministry of Economic Affairs. Significantly, there was hardly any mention of formalised linkages with the private sector or industry.

With regard to the connectedness of development-related activities to the academic core, the articulation and academic ratings applied to the four projects/centres are presented in Figure 10.

FIGURE 10 **Plotting the development-related projects/centres at the University of Dar es Salaam**

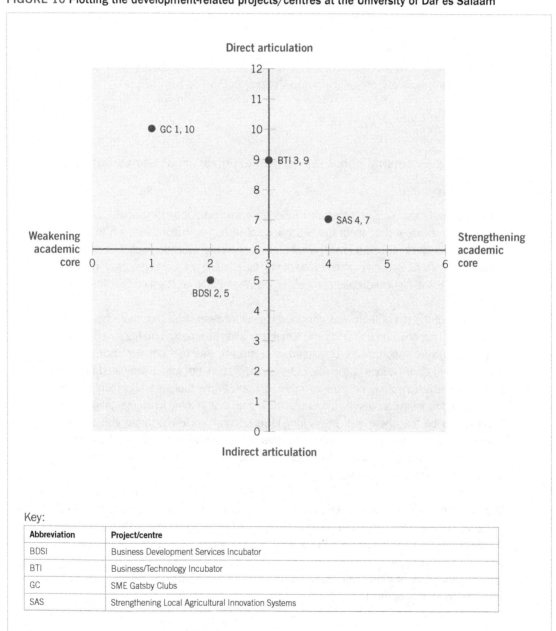

Key:

Abbreviation	Project/centre
BDSI	Business Development Services Incubator
BTI	Business/Technology Incubator
GC	SME Gatsby Clubs
SAS	Strengthening Local Agricultural Innovation Systems

> ### FINDINGS
>
> - Projects/centres that were considered by university leadership to be strongly connected to development tended to score well on the articulation indicators – in other words, they reflected national priorities (and to a lesser extent institutional objectives), had more than one funding source and, in some cases, plans for financial sustainability, and may have had a connection to an implementation agency.
> - However, only one project was rated as strengthening the academic core, indicating something of a disconnect.
> - The Strengthening Local Agricultural Innovation Systems project scored high on both articulation and strengthening the academic core. The challenge is to increase the number of projects that do both.

11.5   Concluding comments about the Tanzania/University of Dar es Salaam case study

There was evidence to suggest that after independence and during the socialist period in Tanzania, there was a pact about the importance of higher education, although there was perhaps a lack of clarity about exactly what the role of higher education was. In addition, it seems that this tacit agreement fragmented during the ensuing political fragmentation and as a result of the 'anti-higher education policies' of the World Bank, amongst other influences.

At the time of the study, there was considerable evidence to show that there was broad agreement at national and university levels that education in general, and higher education in particular, was important for development. However, this had not necessarily been translated into clear notions of the role of higher education, nor into coordinated policies and implementation plans on how to make it work. While there were certainly some capacity and funding constraints, it was also more than that. A more fundamental problem appeared to be that there was not a long-term cultural, socio-economic and political understanding and commitment between universities, political authorities and society at large of the identity or vision of universities, what was expected of universities, and what the rules and values of the universities were.

The academic core of the University of Dar es Salaam had some considerable input strengths on which the institution could build; the challenge will be to translate these into stronger outputs. From the study of the development projects it also seemed that while the projects were strongly articulated to development needs, more could be done to strengthen the academic core of the university, which would enable it to make a more sustainable contribution to development.

12
Uganda
and Makerere University

12.1 The higher education and economic development context in Uganda

How did Uganda fare in meeting the 'preconditions' for an effective and productive relationship between higher education and economic development identified by Pillay's (2010b) investigation of three successful systems?

High-quality schooling: Participation rates were surprisingly low at the secondary level. The gross enrolment ratio in secondary education was 18% in 2006, and the net enrolment ratio 16%. The corresponding averages for sub-Saharan Africa were 32% and 25%, not high by developing country standards (60% and 53%, respectively), but much higher than the Ugandan figures. Moreover, there was considerable concern about inefficiencies in the system, particularly around completion rates at the primary levels and quality of provision and outcomes throughout the system. The survival rate to the last grade of primary schooling was 25% in 2006 (the average for sub-Saharan Africa was 67% and that for developing countries, 81%) (UNESCO 2009).

Effective economic and education planning: There was no official commitment to economic and education planning, although the link between economic development and education, especially tertiary education, was recognised.

The role of the state: The state was playing an important role with respect to funding, as well as encouraging private sector provision of higher education. The state's policy document, the *National Development Plan*, gives some prominence to the role of tertiary education in development. However, financial resource constraints were clearly preventing it from ensuring effective implementation of desired policies.

Partnerships: In general, no evidence could be gleaned of partnerships between the state, the universities and the private sector.

Institutional differentiation: There was evidence of differentiation amongst universities (e.g. Makerere – teaching and research; Mbarara – science and technology; and Kyambogo – teacher and vocational education).

Quality: Serious questions had been raised about the quality of educational provision across the system, resulting particularly from poor internal inefficiency and inadequate funding especially at the secondary and tertiary levels.

Funding: State funding of tertiary education was low in absolute terms given the extent of need and the imperative to increase access and enhance equity.

Innovation: At the time of the study, Uganda had not invested sufficiently either in its universities or its private sector, nor had it provided appropriate incentives for partnerships to develop between these two sets of important actors.

12.2   Evidence of a pact around the role of higher education in Uganda?

Uganda's indicator ratings for the role of knowledge and universities in national and institutional policies and plans are presented in Table 45.

At the national level, the dominant focus of the development approach that both the *Poverty Eradication Action Plan* and the national development plan recognised was the need to eradicate poverty through stimulating and maintaining high levels of economic growth. In order to attain the growth and poverty eradication objectives, the roles of education, broad human capital development, and science and technology were acknowledged.

In addition, it was acknowledged that inadequate human resources and low levels of investment in science and technology were key binding constraints. While there were positive signs of an emerging awareness of the importance of the knowledge economy in new national plans, the role of higher education had not been clarified or agreed upon. This was evident in, amongst others, the low levels of funding and the low higher education participation rates.

At the university (Makerere) level, there was a significant emergence of the narrative of the importance of a knowledge economy amongst university stakeholders, and this was increasingly reflected in institutional policies. There was also a strong orientation towards providing appropriate human resources to the growing economy. Overall, there was a strong development orientation, but this awareness had not yet been institutionalised in policies and structures that could operationalise this new orientation, hence the comment by a senior academic that the university was still in a traditional mode of producing skills for the civil service.

TABLE 45 **Role for knowledge and universities in development in Uganda**

National rating = 4/6			
The concept of a knowledge economy features in the national development plan	3 Strong Appears in a number of policies	**2 Weak** Only mentioned in one policy	1 Absent Not mentioned at all
A role for higher education in development in national policies and plans	3 Prevalent Clearly mentioned in development policies	**2 Weak**	1 Absent
University rating = 5/6			
Concept of a knowledge economy features in institutional policies and plans	**3** Features strongly in strategic plan and/or research policy/strategy	2 Vague reference in strategic plan or research policy	1 Not mentioned at all
Institutional policies with regard to the university's role in economic development	3 Institutional policy	**2** Embedded in strategic plan, research policy, etc.	1 No formal policies

FINDINGS

- At the national level, the importance of the knowledge economy and the importance of higher education were rather weakly reflected in national policy statements.
- In contrast, at the institutional level, there was much stronger reference to the knowledge economy. The important role of the university in development was also in the strategic plan.
- There was no broad agreement between national and institutional levels that knowledge, and by implication higher education, is key to development.

Notions of the role of knowledge and universities in development

Table 46 summarises the notions of the role of higher education held by national and institutional stakeholders, and indicates whether the notion was strong, prevalent, present or absent altogether.

While acknowledging that there is seldom a single notion within the university about the role of higher education, at Makerere there was a very strong emphasis in both the interviews and the key planning and strategy documents that the university must be connected, through its role as the knowledge institution, to national development. The knowledge economy notion ran concurrent with that of the instrument for development notion but, interestingly, the latter was directed at government and business, while there was very little mention of linkages to communities, particularly in the strategic plans.

TABLE 46 **Comparing national and institutional notions of the role of higher education in Uganda**

Notions		National stakeholders		University stakeholders
Ancillary	•	Perception that university is not contributing enough to development	•	Not a self perception of the leadership
Self-governing	☐	This is the traditional role expected of the university	■	Strongly present amongst academics with considerable disquiet about government interference
Instrument for development agendas	■	Very strong expectation of academics to also be development practitioners	■	Particularly poverty reduction and support of local business as experts
Engine for development	•	Recently introduced in the discourse of development plans	☐	Knowledge economy and development discourse is strongly foregrounded in the strategic plan but little evidence of buy-in and implementation

Key:

■ Strong   ☐ Present   • Absent

FINDINGS

- In terms of notions of the role of the university in development, at the national level there was a strong instrumental expectation, with some reference to the autonomy issue.
- At the institutional level, there was a strong leaning towards both instrumental and self-governing notions. There was an increasing awareness of the engine of development approach, particularly at the planning level, but it was not yet dominant amongst the leadership.
- At both the national and the institutional levels the instrumental and self-governing notions were dominant, but not resolved. Amongst university leadership there was an increasing support for a knowledge economy approach.

12.3   The academic core of Makerere University

The analysis of the university's academic core presented in the case study report was undertaken on the basis of the rating of seven key indicators as 'strong', 'medium' or 'weak'. The data on which the ratings are based are contained in the detailed case study report.[23] The seven indicators and their ratings are presented in Table 47.

---

23   The Uganda and Makerere University case study report is available at www.chet.org.za.

TABLE 47 **Makerere University: Rating of the academic core**

	Indicator	Rating (strong/medium/weak)*
1	Science, engineering and technology enrolments and graduations	SET students = 32% in 2007. SET graduation rate for 2007 was 22%
2	Postgraduate/undergraduate enrolments ratio Masters/PhD enrolment ratio	Proportion of postgraduates is 9% in 2007, up from 6% in 2001
3	Teaching load: Academic staff–student ratio	Overall ratio was 1:18 in 2007 and 1:11 for SET
4	Proportion of academic staff with doctorates	31% of permanent academics have a doctorate (2007)
5	Research income per permanent academic staff member**	Low at PPP$ 2 000
6	Doctoral graduates	Graduates in 2007 constituted 2% of permanent academics
7	Research publications	Output in 2007 was 0.20 of publications per permanent academic

Key:

■ Strong   ▨ Medium   □ Weak

* Refer to Appendix F for a detailed descriptions of the academic core rating categories.

** No specific information provided on research funding. All gifts and grants funding assumed to be research income.

The following observations can be made about the academic core data for Makerere University:

1. **SET enrolments**: Makerere had a strong growth in SET enrolments, from 4 400 in 2001 to 11 000 in 2007. But it still had (at 32%) a relatively low proportion of SET enrolments in 2007. Its SET graduation rate was satisfactory.
2. **Postgraduate enrolments**: Makerere's postgraduate enrolment increased between 2001 and 2007, at double the rate of undergraduate enrolments. Its postgraduate percentage of 9% in 2007 was relatively low. Makerere had a strong growth of 15.5% in masters enrolments between 2001 and 2007, but a low growth of only 2.3% in doctoral enrolments. What was of particular concern was Makerere's low proportion of doctoral enrolments relative to its masters enrolments. In 2007 it enrolled only 32 masters students per doctoral enrolment. This suggests that Makerere had a poor flow of students from masters to doctoral studies.
3. **Teaching load**: Makerere's FTE student enrolment grew at a rate which was more than three times higher than its growth in FTE academic staff. This raised its FTE student to FTE staff ratios. In 2007 its student to academic staff ratio in SET was 11:1 and its overall ratio was 18:1. This implies that Makerere's academics had reasonable teaching loads. The average ratio does, however, hide a problematically high FTE student to FTE academic staff ratio of 96:1 in business and management studies.

4. **Qualifications of staff**: In 2007 31% of Makerere's permanent academic staff had doctorates as their highest formal qualifications.
5. **Research funding**: The estimates calculated suggest that the university was not able to fund its research activities adequately.
6. **Doctoral graduates**: Doctoral graduates increased from 11 in 2001 to 23 in 2007, which was a modest 13% increase, and from a very low base. Doctoral enrolments also grew rather slowly, from 28 to 32 over the same period. This was in sharp contrast to the doubling of masters enrolments, from 1 167 to 2 767. The rather low ratio of 2% of doctoral graduates to permanent academic staff meant that the university would have difficulty reproducing itself.
7. **Research outputs**: In terms of publications, Makerere had shown a high growth from 73 units in 2001 to 233 in 2007. But its 2007 ratio of publication units per permanent academic was still, at 0.20, below the ratio of 0.50 which had been set as a target for South Africa's research universities.

In terms of input variables Makerere had a favourable staff teaching load. It fell into the category 'medium' in terms of SET enrolments and proportion of staff with doctorates, but had a weak research income per permanent academic staff member. In terms of output variables such as research output and the production of doctorates, Makerere performed poorly. The two key factors that seemed to be weakening the academic core were the low throughput from masters to doctorates and the low research funding available to permanent academics. Positive developments were the increase in masters students and the tripling of research output, albeit from a low base.

FINDINGS

-   The university was not significantly changing from a predominantly undergraduate teaching institution.
-   On the input side, Makerere scored strongly on only one indicator (staff teaching load) and medium on staff qualifications and postgraduate enrolments (masters courses). However, it scored weak on the knowledge production indicators – doctoral graduation rates and research output.
-   The knowledge production output variables of the academic core did not seem strong enough to enable Makerere to make a sustainable contribution to development.

12.4   Coordination and connectedness

Knowledge policy coordination and implementation

Table 48 presents the ratings for the coordination of knowledge policies at the national level. While there were positive signs of an emerging awareness of the importance of the knowledge economy in new national plans, the role of higher education had not been clarified or agreed upon, and as can be seen from the ratings, economic development and higher education planning were not linked, coordination and consensus building between government agencies was not apparent, the ministry had weak capacity, and there was considerable funding inconsistency. This means that the increasing awareness of the importance of the knowledge economy in development was not yet coordinated or implemented.

TABLE 48 National coordination of knowledge policies in Uganda

National rating = 3/9			
Economic development and higher education planning are linked	3 Systematic Formal structures Headed by senior minister	2 Sporadic Clusters/forums	**1 Weak** Occasional meetings
Link between universities and national authorities	3 Specific coordination structures or agencies	2 Some formal structures but no meaningful coordination	1 No structures, and political rather than professional networks
Coordination and consensus building of government agencies involved in higher education	3 Higher education mainstreamed across government departments	2 Intermittent interaction with ineffective forums	1 Higher education issues limited mainly to one ministry or directorate

FINDINGS

- At the national level, there seemed to be many informal interactions, but no institutionalised processes of coordination.
- While there were considerable personal networks between government officials and particular university leaders, it was not clear whether this was contributing towards building consensus and strengthening the institution.

Table 49 summarises the ratings of the indicators relating to the implementation of knowledge policies and activities at both the national and university levels.

TABLE 49 Implementation of knowledge policies and activities in Uganda

National rating = 6/12		
Role of the ministry responsible for higher education	3 Organised ministry with capacity to make predictable allocations	2 Spots of capacity with some steering instruments	**1** Weak capacity with unpredictable allocations
Implementation to 'steer' higher education towards development	3 Strong Instruments such as funding/ special projects that incentivise institutions/individuals	2 Weak Occasional grants for special projects	**1 Absent** No particular incentive funding
Balance/ratio of sources of income for institutions	**3** Government, fees and third stream	**2** Mainly government plus student fees	1 Mainly government with external funders
Funding consistency	3 A stable, transparent public funding mechanism based on criteria agreed upon by all actors involved	**2** Funding allocations somewhat predictable but do not allow for long-term planning nor reward enterprising behaviour	1 No clear funding or incentives from government
University rating = 10/18		
Specific units, funding or appointments linked to economic development	3 Specific units, funding or appointments	2 Economic development initiatives aspect of a unit or appointment	**1** Mainly ad hoc, staff-initiated operations
Incentives and rewards for development-related activities	3 Incentives/counts towards promotion	**2** Some signals but largely rhetoric	1 No mention
Teaching programmes linked to the labour market	3 Targets for enrolments in fields considered to be of high economic relevance	**2** Some programmes in response to specific industry requests	1 No new programmes linked to labour market
Special programmes linking students to economic development	3 Entrepreneurship, work-based learning and/or incubators for students mainstreamed	2 Ad hoc programmes	**1** No special programmes
Research activities becoming more economy-oriented	**3** Research policy/strategy has an economic development focus	2 Some research agendas have an economic development focus	1 Ad hoc project funding
Levels of government and institutional funding for research	3 High	2 Medium	**1** Low

- At the national level, the Department of Education seemed to have low capacity with no steering mechanisms and somewhat unpredictable funding.
- While the university did have development-related structures and special programmes linking it to development initiatives, the problem was that in too many cases these initiatives were driven by individuals rather than being institutionalised.
- While government support for research was low, the university, within tight budget constraints, was trying to increase research related to development activities. However, research related to development was not significantly rewarded through incentives beyond the traditional academic promotion system.

Makerere University's connectedness to external stakeholders and the academic core

At the institutional level, the third strategic area of Makerere University's strategic plan is "Partnership and Networking". The strategies involved:

- Stakeholder participation in the university policy agenda;
- Collaborating and networking with public and private sector institutions;
- Creating research and technology innovation and incubation business centres;
- Involving public and private sector participation in curricula development;
- Stakeholder participation in planning, supervision and evaluation of the students on field attachment; and
- Creating a resource-pool of university expertise for the use public and private sectors.

However, despite examples of linkages with government and industry (or the private sector) at the level of projects, there was not much evidence of strong engagement with the public and private sectors. While some institutional leaders reported that the university encourages disciplines to form consulting firms, one respondent reported that government frequently used foreign firms rather than locals for consultancies. Another respondent spoke about limited trust between government and the university and that the government did not always recognise the value of the institution.

In summary, there was very little evidence in either the interviews with university stakeholders, or in policy and strategy documents, of strong linkages with government or industry – although there was some evidence of the intention to strengthen these linkages. In addition, there was no evidence of formal structures or platforms for interaction between these role players. The unit responsible for promoting and coordinating linkages with external stakeholders did seem to play an important role in asserting the university's strategic objectives and agenda when negotiating funding with foreign donors.

With regard to the connectedness of development-related activities to the academic core, the articulation and academic ratings applied to the six projects/centres are presented in Figure 11.

FIGURE 11 **Plotting the development-related projects/centres at Makerere University**

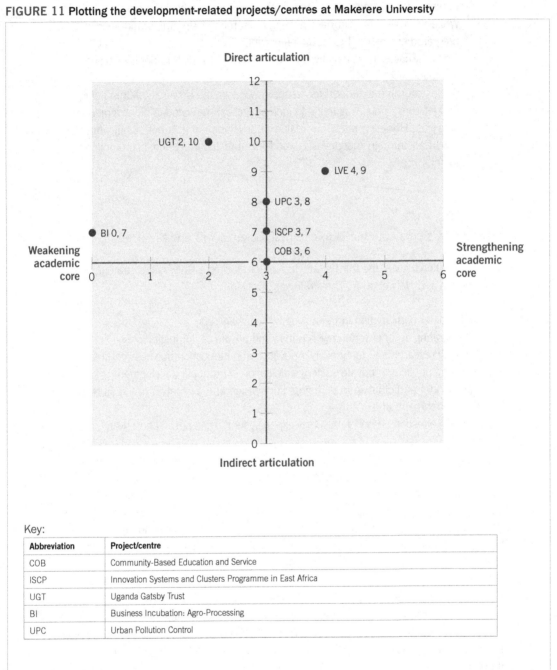

Key:

Abbreviation	Project/centre
COB	Community-Based Education and Service
ISCP	Innovation Systems and Clusters Programme in East Africa
UGT	Uganda Gatsby Trust
BI	Business Incubation: Agro-Processing
UPC	Urban Pollution Control

FINDINGS

- Projects/centres that were considered by university leadership to be strongly connected to development tended to score well on the articulation indicators – in other words, they reflected national priorities (and to a lesser extent institutional objectives), had more than one funding source and, in some cases, plans for financial sustainability, and may have had a connection to an implementation agency.
- However, five out of six of the projects were not rated as strengthening the academic core, indicating something of a disconnect.

12.5 Concluding comments about the Uganda/Makerere University case study

The dominant focus of the development approach that both the *Poverty Eradication Action Plan* and the national development plan recognised was the need to eradicate poverty through stimulating and maintaining high levels of economic growth. In order to attain the growth and poverty eradication objectives, the roles of education, human capital development broadly and science and technology were acknowledged as well as the facts that inadequate human resources and low levels of investment in science and technology were key binding constraints. While there were positive signs of an emerging awareness of the importance of the knowledge economy in new national plans, the role of higher education had not been clarified or agreed upon. This could be seen from the ratings about funding, low participation rates, weak coordination and weak implementation capacity.

Within the recent government and university documents there was recognition of the importance of the knowledge role of the university. In particular, higher education was beginning to be recognised as a contributor to development, and not just as a provider of human resources for the civil service and the professions. However, the government was not investing sufficiently in either the universities or innovation, nor had it provided appropriate incentives for partnerships. Furthermore, this growing development awareness had not been translated into coordinated policies or implementation actions, as both the government and the university were having problems in making tough reallocation decisions. This means that the pact was not strong enough to make unpopular trade-offs, resulting in few real resource re-distributions to implement the changing vision.

The Makerere University academic core had some input strengths on which the institution could build; the challenge will be to translate these into stronger outputs. From the study of the development projects it also seemed that while the projects were strongly articulated to development needs, much more could be done to strengthen the academic core of the university, which will enable it to make a more sustainable contribution to development.

Part 4
CONCLUSIONS
AND IMPLICATIONS

Three years of HERANA research into the role of universities in economic development in Africa, including surveys of three successful innovation-driven OECD countries and eight African nations and universities, produced an analytical framework to explore the role of universities in (economic) development and how this role might be operationalised. It also produced the most comprehensive, systematic and comparative data on a group of sub-Saharan African universities ever compiled.

The research led to key findings in three broad areas, the needs: for a 'pact' that sees governments, universities, funders and other stakeholders agree on a central role for higher education in economic development and the knowledge economy; for strengthening the 'academic core' of universities that is essential to producing knowledge, reproducing the academy and providing the high-level skills that drive development; and for improving policy (and implementation) coordination at national and institutional levels in ways that help to connect universities more effectively to development.

FINDINGS

- There was a lack of clarity and agreement (pact) about a development model and the role of higher education in development, at both national and university levels. There was, however, an increasing awareness, particularly at government level, of the importance of universities in the global context of the knowledge economy.
- Research production at the eight African universities was not strong enough to enable them to build on their traditional undergraduate teaching roles and make a sustainable, comprehensive contribution to development via new knowledge production. A number of universities had manageable student–staff ratios and adequately qualified staff, but inadequate funds for staff to engage in research. In addition, the incentive regimes did not support knowledge production.
- In none of the countries in the sample was there a coordinated effort between government, external stakeholders and the university to systematically strengthen the contribution that the university can make to development. While at each of the universities there were exemplary development projects that connected strongly to external stakeholders and strengthened the academic core, the challenge is how to increase the number of these projects.

Pact needed on 'engine for development' role for universities

The development model of the three OECD systems studied in this project represents what the WEF competitiveness report classifies as 'innovation-driven' – in other words, these countries have agreed that knowledge and education are key productive factors in development. From the sample of eight African countries, three (Mauritius, South Africa and Botswana) were in the 'efficiency' phase, meaning that improved efficiency and higher education and training were increasingly playing an important role in economic development. The other countries were in the process of moving from 'factor' (natural resources and low skills base) towards efficiency and, by implication, an increasing importance for education and training.

This study revealed that the three efficiency-driven systems already had substantially higher participation rates in higher education but that, with the exception of Mauritius, none of the countries had a consistent development model, nor was there agreement that knowledge is a key productive factor. In the rest of the sample there were emerging knowledge policies, but they are located mainly in one government department, with weak coordination and implementation.

In most of the countries in the sample, as a kind of compensation for the absence of a development model, grand, national visions were constructed. These visions, some looking forward as far as 2030, had no implementation plans or systematic monitoring mechanisms. To some extent they could be seen as attempts at constructing a common vision – and by implication confirming that there was no pact.

Mauritius was the only country where, at both the national and institutional levels, there was a belief that knowledge is a key driver of development, and where the government and the institution had similar notions about the role of the university. However, in terms of the academic core, coordination and implementation it did not seem as if the pact had been properly operationalised as yet.

The lack of the pact in our sample countries was also evidenced by the lack of consensus between national and university stakeholders around the role of higher education and universities. Amongst national stakeholders, the dominant expectation was that universities made a direct contribution to development. This instrumental notion emphasises contribution in the form of expertise exchange and capacity building, rather than the production of new scientific knowledge. It was a constant refrain from government stakeholders that universities were not contributing enough to development; however, this was usually in reference to addressing broad social problems rather than to economic development in particular.

On the whole, national stakeholders and some government policies and plans reflected the language of the knowledge economy and the role of the university as the 'engine of development' – more so than university stakeholders and plans did. However, it is likely that this was still a more instrumental notion of knowledge since it was used in the sense of direct application to development issues rather than the more indirect role of knowledge and universities in R&D and innovation.

It is surprising that amongst university leadership, support for the role of the university in the knowledge economy was rather weak. Instead, the two dominant notions reflect the traditional tension between the university as a self-governing institution that indirectly contributes to development, versus a more direct instrumental role. There was an emerging awareness of the importance of an 'engine of development' approach in the sample but, with the exception of Mauritius, it was far from being the dominant view.

In the period following independence in many African countries, a clear pact developed between government and universities that universities would provide the human capital (civil service and professions) for the new states. That pact is long gone. Instead, there are a range of policy visions and notions, often contradictory, within government and within universities about how to respond to changing development demands that are increasingly driven by knowledge. What has not changed is that there was, with the exception of Mauritius, not a generally agreed upon development model, with the result that neither the government nor institutions agreed on the role of higher education in development.

It could thus be argued that there needs to be considerably more emphasis on 'forging' agreement between governments, funders and university leaders that knowledge and higher education are key productive forces. So while capacity-building is important, consensus-building is equally important – capacity-building without agreement on 'capacity for what' may be part of the 'bottomless pit' syndrome in Africa.

A potentially positive development in terms of forging greater agreement across different constituencies is that in all the countries, tertiary or higher education councils had been established, partially to compensate for weak ministries but also to do 'independent' certification and quality assessments. At the time of the study, they were partially 'symptoms' of problems in the system, but all were undergoing 'role re-definitions' and could become key players in promoting discussions about the role of higher education in development and in monitoring progress.

Strengthening the academic core – incentives are key

The university is a specialised institution whose core business is knowledge – its production, reproduction and dissemination. In addition, the university can only participate in the global knowledge economy and make a sustainable contribution to development if its 'academic core' is strong. The core knowledge production output variables of the sample of African universities were not strong enough for them to make a sustainable contribution to development, and the academic core indicators did not show significant signs of strengthening knowledge production outputs (doctorates and publications).

As was the case with the European university tradition before the second world war, and until fairly recently the Latin American model (Swartzman 2010), the universities in our sample were still predominantly organised as undergraduate teaching institutions, despite some rather grandiose mission statements and claims to be knowledge producers. But just as was the case in Europe, Latin America and Asia, the challenges facing African universities are to expand their role beyond teaching to research and to become significant contributors to what Douglass *et al.* (2009: 1) call 'globalisation's muse': 'Universities and higher education systems, for both real and romanticised reasons have become globalisation's muse: in essence a widely recognised route to full participation in the knowledge society.'

The convergence in weakness of research output was in contrast to much greater variance in input strengths. The strongest input indicators were in manageable student–staff ratios and the relatively high level of staff with PhDs, which could partially account for solid undergraduate success rates. However, these success rates have to be seen within the context of the combination of a flagship university in a national system of low participation rates, meaning a very elite group of students.

The two areas of greatest concern on the input side were the low levels of postgraduate students, particularly at the doctorate level, and the lack of research funds. A striking feature of postgraduate enrolment was the dramatic increase in masters enrolments and graduations. There were two sides to this. On the one hand, course work masters degrees certainly contributed to increasing the pool of highly-skilled workers beyond the bachelor degree, which is a feature of many knowledge economies. On the other hand, these mainly course work masters programmes did not seem to prepare students for doctoral studies, particularly the research and dissertation components. Very poor throughput rates – in some cases, more than 50 masters students for every PhD enrolment – attested to this. But there could also be other contributing factors, such as the fact that there were many more scholarships for masters programmes, particularly from foreign donors, while scholarships for doctoral studies were much scarcer.

Not enrolling and graduating PhDs has a number of serious consequences. Firstly, the flagship university has to reproduce its own academic staff, as well as academics for other higher education institutions in the system. It also has to respond to the increasing demand in the knowledge economy for people with doctorates in institutions other than the university, such as research institutes, and for high-level person power in top positions in a range of industrial and financial institutions.

New knowledge production and connecting university research to application and innovation is most frequently led by academic staff with doctorates and research programmes. The vast majority of the development activities identified by university leadership for the study were led by academics with PhDs. Growing the cadre of doctorates is an essential task for a flagship university – not only to reproduce itself, but also to produce knowledge that can connect the institution to both the global knowledge economy and the local community.

'ISI-referenced publications' represents a narrow notion of research which does not reflect research that feeds into application or consultancy, and could thus be seen as only the tip of the 'research iceberg'. However, this is the tip that makes a flagship university part of the global knowledge community, and publishing part of an international disciplinary or inter-disciplinary community. Three crucial components of what might be called an output-oriented research culture that produces the 'tip' are: staff with appropriate research training (having a PhD is an essential but not sufficient requirement), research funding, and a conducive incentive environment.

The first problem with the incentive structure at the university level starts with the problem of very little earmarked research funding coming from government, which puts pressure on universities to find incentive money from their already-stretched budgets. While almost every university had a research fund, the funds had to be shared with related activities such as conference attendance, equipment and information resources. In addition, it seemed that most of these internal 'open competitive' funding sources were mainly incentives for young academics and doctoral students, with many senior academics saying that the amounts available were not worth applying for. A related problem, in some cases, was that while some money was available for equipment, it was nearly impossible to get equipment maintenance funds.

The second problem with the incentives structure is that it seemed a major distraction from PhD supervision and academic research for some staff was multiple private teaching opportunities, both within public institutions with 'private' students and in private higher education institutions located in close proximity to the flagship institution. So while the teaching load, according to student–staff ratios, might not have been excessive, this 'triple teaching' as a form of income supplementation was another contributor to weakening the academic core.

A third potential problem is related to consultancies for government, foreign donors and industry. While most academics interviewed mentioned consultancies, it was very difficult to get anything near an accurate picture of consultancy activity. (In one of the Dar es Salaam annual reports a figure of about 800 consultancies was mentioned.) Nevertheless, what emerged from these discussions was that consultancies had major advantages over research grants. Firstly, it is a personal relationship with a donor that often also has other benefits such as travelling to the donor country and being invited to networks of other recipients. Secondly, consultancies provide both direct supplementation of income and have much greater flexibility about how the funds are spent (whereas research grants often have numerous stipulations about travel, hiring of researchers, buying of equipment, etc.).

It is clear from this investigation that in order to 'refocus' flagship universities, attention will have to be paid to incentive structures that promote knowledge production. Low knowledge production cannot be blamed solely on low capacity and resources. What needs to be incentivised is PhD supervision and research programmes that strengthen the academic core, make these flagship universities part of the global academic community, and connect them to local and regional development.

Part of developing the academic core will be to improve and strengthen the definition of key performance indicators, as well as the systematic, institution-wide capturing and processing (institutionalisation) of key performance indicator data. Such indicators will be key for national and institutional decision-makers to design evidence-based policies and incentives, rather than the current over-reliance on aspirational mission statements.

Coordination and connectedness to development

The university cannot unilaterally strengthen the academic core and connect it to development-related activities. It requires the coordination of government policies and other external stakeholders. At the national level, there were considerable coordination activities in most countries, ranging from forums and clusters to the reorganisation of national ministries. However, this seemed to be mostly weak or 'symbolic' coordination.

Evidence of this was not only in the lack of supporting policies across relevant departments, but also in the focus of such policies often being contingent on the interests of different and changing government ministers. This was reflected, amongst others ways, in the fact that policies to support research were often in departments of science and technology, but not in education. Another indicator was the reconfiguration of ministries of education, either separating higher education from basic education, linking and delinking higher education from science and technology, or even linking higher education to training.

In the absence of a pact, and with competing notions and a lack of consensus between universities, national authorities and external actors about the university's identity and its role in development, coordination becomes virtually impossible. A consequence is that the energy and actions of university leaders and academics have to be invested in continuous, unpredictable negotiations, particularly about funding from government – instead of in strengthening the core academic activities of the institution. The result of this is often fragmented and inefficient organisations characterised by intra-organisational struggles for power, autonomy and funding.

The above can be illustrated by looking at research funding. In all eight countries there were national policies that promote research and innovation, but these were mostly located within science and technology departments, not in education (with the exception of Botswana and Mauritius). Funding from government through education departments was mainly for teaching and infrastructure, with between 1–3% available for research at most institutions. Academics often described their government's contribution to research funds as 'negligible'.[24]

In all the countries studied dissatisfaction was expressed with the national research councils: not only were the amounts of money limited, but funds were cumbersome to access through complicated application procedures, and grants were often for short periods, meaning repeated reapplication.

In the absence of a coordinated funding and incentive strategy from government, reliance on external funding increases which, in turn, can contribute to more fragmentation and 'projectisation'. This weakens the academic core of universities because knowledge is not accumulated and fed into teaching and publishing, and the entire system is more vulnerable to donor agendas, interventions and political interference.

---

24   According to Oyewole (2010), on average, sub-Saharan African countries spend less than 0.3% of their GDP on research – the lowest in the world. Furthermore, Africa has lost 11% of its share of global science since its peak in 1987, while sub-Saharan science has lost almost a third (31%).

Although donor aid in Africa has not reached the ambitious targets set at the 2005 G8 summit, reaching about 60% of the targets still amounts to a significant increase in development aid to Africa in general, and to higher education in particular. The issue is not only about more aid but, equally importantly, how to spend the aid more effectively.

This study shows that the coordination of agendas and projects with donors is a major problem, not to mention the considerable administrative effort required for accounting to multiple donors. Only two universities (Dar es Salaam and Eduardo Mondlane) had established strong donor coordination structures. But, as was indicated in the case of Eduardo Mondlane, to strengthen the academic core requires coordination and a joint effort by donors and government; research and doctoral training cannot be 'outsourced' to donors while government funds undergraduate teaching.

One way to start addressing the serious shortage and lack of coordination of national and continental research funds, is to consider an African version of the European Research Council, a body that concentrates large amounts of funds to promote frontier research excellence.

Strengthening the academic core not only requires more research funds but also mechanisms that connect the university to development activities in ways that strengthen rather than weaken the academic core. Starting with industry linkages, while there was evidence of connecting to industry or the private sector in all eight universities, this was generally confined to the level of units or centres rather than institutional-level partnerships. Except for ad hoc consultancies at some universities, there was hardly any evidence of university engagement in R&D with, or for, industry.

To a large extent this is because the industrial sector in most of the African countries studied is largely under-developed, and because there is very limited private sector R&D – where global companies do have operations in the African countries, their R&D is usually undertaken elsewhere. This is a problem in most developing countries but it is particularly acute in Africa. However, some of the universities are beginning to address the lack of interaction between their institutions and industry or the private sector through the establishment of university–industry liaison structures.

Interaction with the private sector took mainly two forms. The first was in the area of education and training. Examples included the use of people from the private sector on advisory committees responsible for curricula design and revision, for work placements, and for specific, customised training programmes. The second form of interaction, at almost all the universities, was business development and support for SMEs. A challenge will be to increase the scale of these initiatives while still connecting them to research and postgraduate training, because these types of projects lend themselves to individual consultancies.

The survey of 44 projects/centres identified by university leaders as being strongly connected to development, ranged from long-term research programmes to postgraduate training and short-term support services to external groupings. At each of the universities there were 'exemplary' development projects/centres that were strongly connected to national/local priorities, had more than one funding source and, in some cases, had a connection to an implementation agency. At the same time, they were strengthening the academic core through training postgraduate students, were part of international academic networks, and had published in peer-reviewed journals and books. A few projects were world class in terms of international recognition and cutting-edge research (particularly in the areas of the environment and health). The challenge is to vastly increase the number and the scale of these types of projects.

Finally, our approach to higher education and development can be illustrated by a version of the Burton Clark 'coordination triangle'. Clark's seminal book *The Higher Education System* (1983) addressed the issue of the organisation of higher education systems and argued that factors that integrate higher education systems (i.e. that keep them from falling apart) are the three forces of coordination: the state, the market and the academic oligarchy. These form the three nodes in his triangle.

In the context of this study, we adapted Clark's triangle (Figure 12) to depict the three main nodes as government, universities and external groupings. These in turn reflect the dynamics of our analytical framework which can be articulated as follows: in order for universities to make a sustainable contribution to development, there needs to be agreement amongst the major actors (a pact) about the role of development; there needs to be capacity in the academic core of universities; and there needs to be coordination and connectedness of the policies and activities of government, universities and external groupings.

These three aspects are interrelated. Without a pact, coordination becomes almost impossible. Without national policies and implementation of these policies, it is very difficult for the university to develop a strong academic core (particularly in developing countries where the market is weak). But, strong academic capacity without being connected to development activities results in the insulation of the university (the 'ivory tower'). Strong connectedness of universities to development, but with weak academic capacity, diminishes the contribution the university can make to development.

The above does not mean that there is one best practice model to achieve this. Our study of the three systems that have been successful in different ways in connecting higher education to development (Finland, South Korea and North Carolina) showed this.

For African countries to move from being providers of raw materials and receivers of foreign aid to the next stages of development that will make them part of the global knowledge economy, implies at least the following. Firstly, agreement (a pact) about the importance of knowledge in development and the special role of the university. Secondly, strengthening the academic core, particularly in terms of knowledge production. Thirdly, greater coordination amongst an increasing number of actors and agencies (multiple government departments, business and foreign donors) involved in higher education. And finally, ensuring that development activities strengthen rather than weaken academic capacity, particularly for flagship universities.

FIGURE 12 The dynamics of the relationship between the pact, academic core and coordination

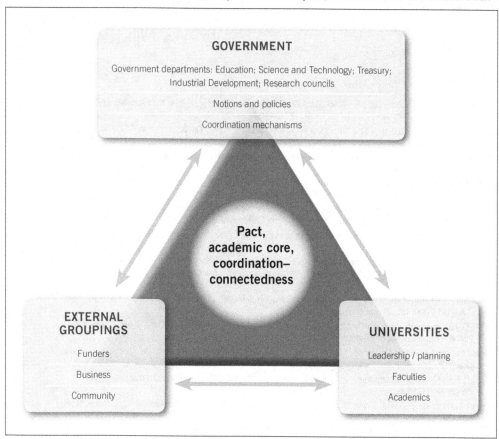

List of sources

Altbach PG and Balán J (eds) (2007) *World Class Worldwide: Transforming research universities in Asia and Latin America.* Baltimore: The Johns Hopkins University Press

Bloom D, Canning D and Chan K (2006) *Higher Education and Economic Development in Africa.* Washington DC: The World Bank

Braun D (2008) Organising the political coordination of knowledge and innovation policies. *Science and Public Policy,* 35(4): 227–239

Brock-Utne B (2002) Formulating higher education policies in Africa: The pressure from external forces and the neo-liberal agenda. *Journal of Higher Education in Africa,* (1)1: 24–56

Carnoy M, Castells M, Cohen SS and Cardoso FH (1993) *The New Global Economy in the Information Age: Reflections on our changing world.* University Park: Pennsylvania State University Press

Castells M (1991) *The University System: Engine of development in the new world economy.* Washington DC: The World Bank

Castells M (2002) Universities as dynamic systems of contradictory functions. In: Muller J, Cloete N and Badat S (eds) *Challenges of Globalisation: South African debates with Manuel Castells.* Cape Town: Maskew Miller Longman

Castells M (2009) Transcript of a lecture on higher education delivered at the University of the Western Cape, 7 August 2009. http://www.chet.org.za/seminars/

CHET (2010) *Cross-national higher education performance indicators.* Draft report. Cape Town: Centre for Higher Education Transformation

Clark B (1983) *The Higher Education System: Academic organization in cross-national perspective.* Berkeley: University of California Press

Clark B (1998) *Creating Entrepreneurial Universities: Organisational pathways of transformation.* Oxford: Pergamon-IAU Press

Coleman J and Court D (1993) *University Development in the Third World: The Rockefeller experience.* New York: Pergamon

Douglass JA, King CJ and Feller I (2009) *Globalization's Muse: Universities and higher education systems in a changing world.* Berkeley: Public Policy Press, Center for Studies in Higher Education, Institute of Governmental Studies

Economic Commission for Africa (2004) *Economic Report on Africa: Unlocking Africa's Trade Potential in the Global Economy Overview.* Twenty-third meeting of the Committee of Experts of the Conference of African Ministers of Finance, Planning and Economic Development, Kampala, Uganda. http://www.uneca.org/cfm/2004/overview.htm

French Academy of Sciences (2006) *Science and Developing Countries: Sub-Saharan Africa.* Paris.

G8 Gleneagles (2005) *The Gleneagles Communiqué.* http://www.chet.org.za/files/reports/Gleneagles_Communique_Africa.pdf

Gastfriend D and Morton R (2010) Promises and plans: An analysis of G8 aid to Africa. *International Institute for Justice and Development (IIJD) Newsletter,* July 2010. http://www.iijd.org/

Gibbons M, Limoges C, Nowotny H, Schwartsman S, Scott P and Trow M (1994) *The New Production of Knowledge: The dynamics of science and research in contemporary societies.* California: Sage

Gornitzka Å, Maassen P, Olsen JP and Stensaker B (2007) 'Europe of knowledge': Search for a new pact. In: P Maassen and JP Olsen (eds), *University Dynamics and European Integration.* Dordrecht: Springer

Hölttä S and Malkki P (2000) *Response of Finnish higher education institutions to the national information society programme.* Helsinki University of Technology

INSEAD (2010) *Global Innovation Index Report 2009–2010.* INSEAD Business School

Juma C and Yee-Cheong L (2005) *Innovation: Applying knowledge in development.* London: Earthscan

Kamara A and Nyende L (2007) Growing a Knowledge-Based Economy: Public expenditure on education in Africa. *Economic Research Working Paper,* No. 88. Tunisia: African Development Bank

Langa PV (2010) Disciplines and engagement in African universities: A study of scientific capital and academic networking in the social sciences. Unpublished PhD Dissertation, University of Cape Town

Maassen P and Cloete N (2006) Global reform trends in higher education. In: N Cloete, R Fehnel, P Maassen, T Moja, H Perold and T Gibbon (eds), *Transformation in Higher Education: Global pressures and local realities.* Second edition. Dordrecht: Springer

Maassen P, Pinheiro R and Cloete N (2007) *Bilateral country investments and foundations partnership projects to support higher education across Africa*. Report commissioned by the US Partnership for Higher Education in Africa. Cape Town: Centre for Higher Education Transformation

Maassen P and Olsen J (2007) University dynamics and European integration. *Higher Education Dynamics*, 19

MacGregor K (2009a) 'Conference calls for higher education action.' *University World News*, 22 July 2009. http://www.universityworldnews.com/article.php?story=20090709193555377

MacGregor K (2009b) 'Africa: Call for higher education support fund.' *University World News*, 22 July 2009. http://www.universityworldnews.com/article.php?story=20090322082237425

MacGregor K (2010) 'Higher education a driver of the MDGs.' *University World News*, 2 May 2010. http://www.universityworldnews.com/article.php?story=20100501081126465

MacGregor K and Makoni M (2010) 'Universities must be citadels not silos.' *University World News*, 2 May 2010. http://www.universityworldnews.com/article.php?story=20100502103801345

Mamdani M (2008) *Scholars in the Marketplace: The dilemmas of neo-liberal reform at Makerere University 1989–2005*. Pretoria: HSRC Press

Moja T, Muller J and Cloete N (1996) Towards new forms of regulation in higher education: The case of South Africa. *Higher Education* 32(2): 129–155

Oyewole O (2010) Africa and the global knowledge domain. In: D Teferra and H Greijn (eds), *Higher Education and Globalization: Challenges, threats and opportunities for Africa*. The Netherlands: Maastricht University Centre for International Cooperation in Academic Development

Pillay P (2010a) *Higher Education and Economic Development: A literature review*. Cape Town: Centre for Higher Education Transformation

Pillay P (2010b) *Linking Higher Education and Economic Development: Implications for Africa from three successful systems*. Cape Town: Centre for Higher Education Transformation

Psacharopoulos G, Tan JP and Jimenez E (1986) *The Financing of Education in Developing Countries: Exploration of policy options*. Washington DC: The World Bank

Santiago P, Tremblay K, Basri E and Arnal E (2008) *Tertiary Education for the Knowledge Society. Volume 1*. Paris: Organisation for Economic Co-operation and Development

Sawyerr A (2004) *Challenges Facing African Universities: Selected issues*. Accra: Association of African Universities

Scott WR (2001) *Organizations: Rational, natural, and open systems*. Upper Saddle River, NJ: Pearson

Sen A (1999) *Development as Freedom*. Oxford: Oxford University Press

Serageldin I (2000) University governance and the stakeholder society. Keynote Address, 11th General Conference: Universities as Gateway to the Future, Durban, 20–25 August 2000, International Association of Universities

Swartzman S (2010) *Changing Universities and Academic Outreach*. Rio de Janeiro: IETS

UNDP (1990) *Human Development Report 1990*. New York: United Nations Development Programme

UNDP (2009) *Human Development Report 2009. Overcoming Barriers: Human mobility and development*. New York: United Nations Development Programme

UNESCO (2009) *EFA Global Monitoring Report 2008*. Paris: United Nations Educational, Scientific and Cultural Organisation

University of Botswana (2008) *University research strategy*. University of Botswana

US Congress (1994) *Higher Education in Africa: Hearing before the subcommittee on African affairs*. 17 May 1993. Washington: US Government Printing Office

WEF (2009) *The Global Competitiveness Report 2009–2010*. Geneva: World Economic Forum

WEF (2010) *The Global Competitiveness Report 2010–2011*. Geneva: World Economic Forum

Weick K (1976) Educational organisations as loosely coupled systems. *Administrative Science Quarterly*, 21:1–19

World Bank (1999) **Knowledge for Development**. *World Development Report 1998/99*. The World Bank Group. Oxford: Oxford University Press

World Bank (2002) *Constructing Knowledge Societies: New challenges for tertiary education*. Washington DC: The World Bank

World Bank (2007) *The Knowledge Economy*. Washington DC: The World Bank

World Bank (2009) *Accelerating Catch-up: Tertiary education for growth in sub-Saharan Africa*. Washington DC: The World Bank

Yesufu TM (ed.) (1973) *Creating the African University: Emerging issues of the 1970s*. Ibadan: Oxford University Press

Appendix A
A higher education and development profile of the countries

For many years, economic development was measured in terms of GDP. Long advocated by international agencies such as the World Bank during most of the second half of the 20th Century, this view argued that the sole concern of developing economies should be to generate high rates of economic growth, which would then permeate through a so-called 'trickle-down' effect to groups at the lower-end of the socio-economic ladder.

However, this rather narrow conception of economic development was broadened by the United Nations Development Programme (UNDP) to include human development and equity. In the *Human Development Report 1990,* human development is defined as 'the process of enlarging people's (basic) choices' (UNDP 1990). In subsequent Human Development Reports, the UNDP refined and extended the concept of 'human development' to include four basic components, of which the first is key – improved health, knowledge and skills – so that people can increase their productivity and participate fully in income-generation and remunerative employment.

From this emerged the Human Development Index (HDI) as a general measure of human development. The HDI is a composite of three basic components of human development: longevity, education and living standards. These components are expressed via the index of life expectancy at birth, the education index (measured by a combination of adult literacy and the combined gross enrolment ratio at primary, secondary and tertiary levels), and the GDP index (measured by real per capita GDP converted to US dollars or international dollars using purchasing power parity).

The human development perspective incorporates, to a large extent, the 'capabilities' approach' to development espoused by Amartya Sen (see Sen 1999, for example). Sen argues that in analysing social justice, there is a strong case for judging individual advantage in terms of the capabilities that a person has. In this perspective, poverty must be seen as the deprivation of basic capabilities rather than merely 'lowness of incomes', which is the standard criterion of identification of poverty. This perspective of capability does not involve any denial of the view that low income is clearly one of the major causes of poverty, and hence under-development, since lack of income can be a principal reason for a person's capability deprivation.

So what are the levels of growth in the sample countries (expressed as GDP per capita)? And, more importantly, to what extent has this growth been translated into human development?

Table A1 compares GDP per capita to the HDI for the eight African countries as well as the three international case study countries. The difference between the GDP per capita and HDI rankings is also calculated (last column). The difference between these two rankings reflects the divergence between economic and broader social development, and is often a consequence of inequality in access to income, education, health, etc. For example, South Africa's HDI ranking is 51 places lower than its GDP per capita ranking, and Botswana's is 65 places lower – these figures are amongst the highest for the countries ranked in this report. Mauritius also exhibits a significant negative difference suggesting that equity may not be such a clearly defined outcome as the policies of the government imply. By contrast, in Finland and South Korea, the HDI ranking is greater than the GDP per capita ranking, suggesting a more holistic pattern of development with lower levels of social inequality. This is also true for Ghana, Kenya, Uganda and Tanzania but at much lower levels of development.

TABLE A1 **Gross domestic product (GDP) per capita vs. Human Development Index (HDI)**

Country	GDP per capita (PPP, USD)* 2007	GDP ranking	HDI Ranking (2007)**	GDP ranking per capita minus HDI ranking
Botswana	13 604	60	125	-65
Ghana	1 334	153	152	1
Kenya	1 542	149	147	2
Mauritius	11 296	68	81	-13
Mozambique	802	169	172	-3
South Africa	9 757	78	129	-51
Uganda	1 059	163	157	6
Tanzania	1 208	157	151	6
Finland	34 526	23	12	11
South Korea	24 801	35	26	9
United States	45 592	9	13	-4

Source: UNDP (2009)

Notes:

* PPP (purchasing power parity) shows a rate of exchange that accounts for price differences across countries, allowing international comparisons of output and incomes. In the table above, PPP USD 1 has the same purchasing power in the domestic economy as USD 1 has in the US.

** 177 countries were ranked.

Table A2 presents a selection of figures which highlight some aspects of the link between higher education and economic development. The most consistent correlation is between participation rate and stage of development; the higher the participation rate, the higher the stage of development. This shows at minimum that even if increasing participation rate is not a sufficient condition, it is at least necessary to change stage of development!

The table also shows that quality of schooling is important, with some exceptions. South Africa has the worst ranking of school quality, but nevertheless the highest competitiveness ranking of the African group – perhaps just another symptom of South Africa also having the highest GDP-HDI discrepancy. Kenya on the other hand has a quality of school system ranking much higher than South Korea and the US, but a very poor competitiveness ranking. The WEF ascribes this largely to weak institutional infrastructure (a code word for politics).

TABLE A2 Selected higher education and economic development indicators

Country	Stage of development (2009–2010)[1]	Quality of education system ranking (2009–2010)[2]	Gross tertiary education enrolment rate (2008)	Overall global competitiveness ranking (2010–2011)[2]
Ghana		71	6.2[5]	114
Kenya		32	4.1[6]	106
Mozambique	Stage 1: Factor-driven	81	1.5[3]	131
Tanzania		99	1.5[5]	113
Uganda		72	3.7	118
Botswana	Transition from 1 to 2	48	7.6[4]	76
Mauritius		50	25.9	55
South Africa	Stage 2: Efficiency-driven	130	15.44	54
Finland		6	94.4	7
South Korea	Stage 3: Innovation-driven	57	98.1	22
United States		26	82.9	4

Source: WEF (2010)

Notes:

[1] Income thresholds (GDP per capita in USD) for establishing stages of development (WEF 2010: 10): Stage 1 Factor-driven: <2 000; Transition from stage 1 to stage 2: 2 000–3 000; Stage 2 Efficiency-driven: 3 000–9 000; Transition from stage 2 to stage 3: 9 000–17 000; Stage 3 Innovation-driven: >17 000.

[2] Ranked out of 139 countries.

[3] 2005 figure.

[4] 2006 figure. The 2010 figure by the Botswana Tertiary Education Council is over 20% while in South Africa the figure remained around 16%.

[5] 2007 figure.

[6] 2009 figure.

The WEF defines 'competitiveness' as 'the set of institutions, policies, and factors that determine the level of productivity of a country' (WEF 2009: 4). The Global Competitiveness Index is based on 12 pillars of competitiveness further divided into three pillar groups, which are:

- Basic requirements (institutions, infrastructure, macro-economic stability, health, primary education);

- Efficiency enhancers (higher education and training, goods market efficiency, labour market efficiency, financial market sophistication, technological readiness, market size); and
- Innovation and sophistication factors (business sophistication, innovation).

The Global Competitiveness Index report regards higher education and training as an important factor in helping countries move towards a knowledge economy (WEF 2009: 5):

> *Quality higher education and training is crucial for economies that want to move up the value chain beyond simple production processes and products. In particular, today's globalising economy requires economies to nurture pools of well-educated workers who are able to adapt rapidly to their changing environment. This pillar measures secondary and tertiary enrollment rates as well as the quality of education as assessed by the business community. The extent of staff training is also taken into consideration because of the importance of vocational and continuous on-the-job training – which is neglected in many economies – for ensuring a constant upgrading of workers' skills to the changing needs of the evolving economy.*

In 2007, the World Bank's report *The Knowledge Economy* identified three main messages. These included the following:

- **Message 1**: Knowledge and innovation have played a crucial role in development from the beginnings of human history. But with globalisation and the technological revolution of the last few decades, knowledge has clearly become the key driver of competitiveness and is now profoundly reshaping the patterns of the world's economic growth and activity. Both developed and developing countries should therefore think, with some urgency, 'about their future under a [knowledge economy] heading'.
- **Message 2**: To become successful knowledge economies, countries have to rethink and act simultaneously on their education base, their innovation systems, and their information and communication technology infrastructure, while also building a high quality economic and institutional regime. Policies for these four pillars have to reflect the country's level of development and will often have to be gradual. However, experience shows that some successful knowledge economy champions have been able to achieve spectacular leaps forward within a decade.
- **Message 3**: Many if not most of the countries that have made rapid progress have staged nationwide knowledge economy-inspired programmes of change. Such programmes have been pragmatic and country-specific, yet some common points emerge: the need to promote trust and social cohesion around the knowledge economy programme; the need to work at the four pillars through a combination of top-down reforms and bottom-up initiatives; and the need for a well-communicated knowledge economy vision.

Appendix B
List of interviewees

BOTSWANA

University of Botswana: Dr Dawid Katzke (Deputy Vice-Chancellor: Finance and Administration), Prof. Isaac Mazonde (Director: Research and Development), Prof. MB Khonga (Dean: Botswana College of Agriculture), Prof. B Tsie (Dean: Faculty of Social Sciences), Prof. Herman Batibo (UB-Tromso Basarwa Research Programme), Dr MMM Bolaane (UB-Tromso Basarwa Research Programme), Prof. B Chilisa (Principal Investigator: UB-UPENN HIV Study), Dr Jennifer Hays (UB-Tromso Basarwa Research Programme), Dr Kapunda (Department of Economics), Dr G Mookodi (Head: Department of Sociology), Prof. N Narayana (Acting Head: Department of Economics), Dr Gabo Ntseane (Head: Department of Adult Education), Mr EDM Odirile (UB Business Clinic, Faculty of Business), Prof. EK Quansah (UB Legal Clinic), Dr Wapula Raditloaneng (Department of Adult Education) and Prof. Siphambe (Department of Economics).

National stakeholders: Sebolaaphuti Kutlwano (Ministry of Finance and Development Planning) and Mr Richard Neill (Director: Policy and Planning, Tertiary Education Council).

GHANA

University of Ghana: Prof. Kwesi Yankah (Pro Vice-Chancellor), Prof. Esi-Sutherland-Addy (Institute of African Studies), Prof. Benjamin Ahunu (Provost: College of Agriculture and Consumer Science), Prof. Sam Offei (Associate Director: West Africa Centre for Crop Improvement), Mr Joseph Budu (Registrar: College of Agriculture and Consumer Science), Prof. Yaa Ntiamoah (Director: School of Research and Graduate Studies), Prof. Eric Danquah (Director: West Africa Centre for Crop Improvement), Dr Vernon Gracen (Associate Director: West Africa Centre for Crop Improvement), Prof. Kodjo Senah (Head: Department of Sociology), Prof. Isabella Quakyi (Principal Investigator: Gates Institute Partnership Projects for Population, Family and Reproductive Health), Prof. Alexander Nyarko (Director: West African Centre for International Parasite Control), Prof. Clement Ahiadeke (Deputy Director: Institute of Statistical Social and Economic Research), Dr Owuraku Sakyi-Dawson (Faculty of Agriculture) and Dr Esi Colecraft (Department of Nutrition and Food Science).

National stakeholders: Ministry of Education, National Council for Tertiary Education, Ministry of Finance and Economic Planning, National Development Planning Commission.

KENYA

University of Nairobi: Mr Ben Waweru (Academic Registrar), Prof. IM Mbeche (Principal: College of Humanities and Social Sciences), Prof. EHN Njeru (Dean: Faculty of Arts), Prof. Edward K Mburugu (Associate Dean: Faculty of Arts), Prof. Patts Odira (Dean: School of Engineering), Prof. Madara Ogot (Managing Director: University of Nairobi Enterprises and Services), Prof. Eric O Odada (Programme Director: Pan African START Secretariat), Prof. Dorothy McCormick (Institute for Development Studies), Mr John Njoka (Institute for Development Studies), Prof. Winnie Mitullah (Institute for Development Studies), Prof. NJ Muthama (Department of Meteorology), Prof. Francis Mutua (Hydrometrology and Surface Water Resources Unit), Prof. Njuguna Ng'ethe (Chronic Poverty Research Centre), Prof. John H Ndiritu (Dean: Faculty of Agriculture), Dr Wanjiru Gichuhi (Population Studies and Research Institute) and Mr Samuel W Kiiru (Institute for Development Studies).

National stakeholder: Elizabeth Wafula (Senior Assistant Commission Secretary (Planning): Commission for Higher Education).

MAURITIUS

University of Mauritius: Prof. I Fagoonee (Vice-Chancellor), Prof. Ameenah Gurib-Fakim (Pro Vice-Chancellor: Teaching and Learning), Prof. Soonil Rughooputh (Pro Vice-Chancellor: Research, Consultancy and Innovation), Prof. K Sobhee (Dean: Faculty of Social Studies and Humanities), Prof. T Bahorun (Department of Biosciences, Faculty of Science), Prof. D Jhurry (Department of Chemistry, Faculty of Science), Dr A Bhaw-Luximon (Department of Chemistry, Faculty of Science), Dr Dinesh Hurreeram (Department of Mechanical and Production Engineering, Faculty of Engineering), Mr I Koodoruth (Senior Lecturer: Department of Social Studies, Faculty of Social Studies and Humanities), Mr A Chutoo (Department of Computer Science and Engineering, Faculty of Engineering), Mr M Santally (Virtual Centre for Innovative Learning Technologies), Mr B Rajkomar (Senior Lecturer: Department of Agricultural Economics and Management, Faculty of Agriculture) and Dr V Ancharaz (Head: Department of Economics and Statistics, Faculty of Social Studies and Humanities).

National stakeholders: Mr Ricaud G Auckbur (Director: Post-secondary and Tertiary, Ministry of Education, Culture and Human Resources), Ms Maya Soonarane (Acting Director: Planning and Finance, Ministry of Education, Culture and Human Resources), Mr R Hittoo (Sector Ministry Support Team Leader for Education Empowerment: Ministry of Finance and Economic Empowerment), Dr Praveen Mohadeb (Tertiary Education Commission) and Mr S Rama (Principal Financial Analyst: Ministry of Finance and Economic Empowerment).

MOZAMBIQUE

Eduardo Mondlane University: Prof. Angêlo Macuacua (Deputy Vice-Chancellor: Management

Affairs), Prof. Orlando Quilambo (Deputy Dean: Academic Affairs), Dr Maria da Conceição (UEM Coordinator for SIDA/SAREC Cooperation), Dr Lidia Brito (Department of Wood Science and Technology), Dr Domingos Buque (Deputy Dean for Research and Postgraduation: Faculty of Education), Prof. António Cumbane (Head: Dept of Chemical Engineering), Prof. Amália Uamasse (Dean: Faculty of Science), Prof. Daniel Baloi (Dean: Faculty of Economics), Prof. Mário Falcão (Dean: Faculty of Agronomy), Prof. Armindo Ngunga (Director: Centre for African Studies), Prof. Manoela M Sylvestre (Director: School of Management and Entrepreneurship in Chibuto), Dr Álvaro Carmo Vaz (retired, Faculty of Engineering), Dr Afonso Lobo (Deputy Dean for Management: Faculty of Engineering), Prof. Boaventura Cuamba (Department of Physics), Prof. Serafina Vilanculos (Faculty of Engineering) and Prof. Brazao Mazula (Faculty of Education).

National stakeholders: Dr Venâncio Simão Massingue (Minister of Science and Technology), Constantino Gode (Advisor: Minister of Finance), Augusto Sumburane (National Director: Ministry of Finance Research Unit), Dr Vitória Afonso de Jesus (National Programme Coordinator: Programa Vilas de Milenio) and Dr Arlindo Chilundo (Advisor: Minister of Education and Culture).

SOUTH AFRICA

Nelson Mandela Metropolitan University: Prof. Derrick Swartz (Vice-Chancellor), Prof. Christo van Loggerenberg (Deputy Vice-Chancellor: Academic), Prof. Thoko Mayekiso (Deputy Vice-Chancellor: Research, Technology and Planning), Prof. Heather Nel (Director: Institutional Planning), Prof. Piet Naude (Director: Business School), Prof. Peter Cunningham (Head: Department of Sociology), Prof. Richard Haines (Professor: Development Studies), Prof. Hendrik Lloyd (Director: School for Economics, Development and Tourism), Ms Jackie Barnett (Director: Innovation, Support and Technology), Prof. Werner Olivier (Head: Department of Mathematics and Applied Mathematics), Prof. Danie Hattingh (Head: Automotive Components Technology Station), Ms Lucinda Lindsay (Researcher: Automotive Components Technology Station), Mr Andrew Young (Researcher: Automotive Components Technology Station), Prof. Hennie van As (Director: Institute for Sustainable Government and Development), Mr Xola Mkontwana (Centre Manager: Small Business Unit), Prof. Jan Neethling (Project Leader: Pebble Bed Modular Reactor project), Prof. Japie Engelbrecht (Project Leader: Pebble Bed Modular Reactor project), Prof. Ben Zeelie (InnoVenton, Institute of Chemical Technology), Geoff Ritson (InnoVenton Technology Support), Dr Willem van Heerden (Dept of Agriculture and Game Management), Prof. JJ van Wyk (Department of Building and Quantity Surveying) and Mr Hugh Bartis (Head: Department of Tourism).

TANZANIA

University of Dar es Salaam: Prof. MAH Maboko (Deputy Vice-Chancellor: Academic Affairs), Dr Sylvia Shayo Temu (Director: Planning and Finance), Prof. C Mwinyiwiwa (Acting Director: Research), Prof. FW Mtalo (Principal: College of Engineering and Technology), Dr Ulingeta Mbamba (Associate Dean: University of Dar es Salaam Business

School), Ms Katherine Fulgence (Business Development Service Incubation Programme), Dr AT Kamukuru (Faculty of Aquatic Sciences and Technology), Dr Cuthbert Kimambo (Business Technology Incubation, College of Engineering and Technology), Prof. NN Luanda (Dept of History, College of Arts and Social Sciences), Dr AE Majule (Institute of Resource Assessment), Dr Daniel Mkude (Department of Linguistics), Dr CL Nahonyo (Head: Department of Zoology), Dr Simon Ndaro (Kinondoni Integrated Coastal Area Management Programme, Faculty of Aquatic Sciences and Technology), Prof. James Ngana (Institute of Resource Assessment), Dr AK Temu (Tanzania Gatsby Trust, College of Engineering and Technology) and Mr Elia Yobu (Programme Officer: University of Dar es Salaam Entrepreneurship Centre).

National stakeholders: Wilbard Abeli (Director for Higher Education: Ministry of Education and Vocational Training), Fatima Kiongosya (Director of Planning: Ministry of Finance and Economic Affairs), Dr Bohela Lunogelo (Executive Director: Economic and Social Research Foundation), Mr Daniel Magwiza (Deputy Secretary: Grants, Finance and Administration, Tanzania Commission for Universities), Prof. MH Nkunya (Executive Director: Tanzania Commission for Universities), Denis Rweyemamu (REPOA – Research on Poverty Alleviation) and Grace Shirima (Ministry of Education and Vocational Training).

UGANDA

Makerere University: Dr Lillian Tibatemwa-Ekirikubinza (Deputy Vice-Chancellor: Academic Affairs), Prof. Eli Katunguka-Rwakishaya (Director: School of Graduate Studies), Mr JW Wabwire (Department of Planning and Development), Ms Florence Nakayiwa-Mayega (Department of Planning and Development), Prof. N Sewankambo (Principal: College of Health Sciences), Dr B Nawangwe (Dean: Faculty of Technology), Prof. Stephen Kijjambu (Dean: School of Medicine), Prof. Edward Kirumira (Dean: Faculty of Social Sciences), Dr Umaru Bagampadde (Head: Department of Civil Engineering), Prof. Sam Kyamanywa (Faculty of Agriculture), Dr Yasin Nakku Ziraba (Faculty of Technology), Ms Grace Twinamatsiko (Faculty of Technology), Dr Frederick Muyodi (Faculty of Science), Dr Joseph Byaruhanga (Uganda Gatsby Trust), Dr John Muyonga (Department of Food Science and Technology), Dr Dorothy Nakimbugwe (Department of Food Science and Technology), Dr Charles Niwagaba (Department of Civil Engineering), Dr Celestino Obua (Department of Pharmacology and Therapeutics), Dr Andrew Mwanika (Faculty of Medicine), Dr Leah Thayer (Infectious Diseases Institute), Prof. Richard Odoi (Department of Pharmacy) and Dr Juliet Kiguli (School of Public Health).

National stakeholders: Dr Evarist Twimukye (Economic Policy Research Centre, Ministry of Finance, Planning and Economic Development), Nyende Magidu (Economic Policy Research Centre, Ministry of Finance, Planning and Economic Development), Prof. ABK Kasozi (Executive Director: National Council for Higher Education), Ms Elizabeth Gabona (Commissioner for Higher Education: Ministry of Education and Sports), Mr Robert Odok Oceng (Visitation Committee to Public Universities, Ministry of Education and Sports), Mrs Rosseti Nabbumba Nayenga (Head of Poverty Desk: Ministry of Finance, Planning and Economic Development).

Appendix C
Indicators of pact, coordination and implementation

TABLE C1 **A role for knowledge and universities in development**

		STRONG	WEAK	ABSENT
National	The concept of a knowledge economy features in the national development plan	Appears in a number of policies	Only mentioned in one policy document	Not mentioned at all
	A role for higher education in development in national policies and plans	Clearly mentioned in development policies		
Institutional	Concept of a knowledge economy features in institutional policies and plans	Features strongly in strategic plan and/or research policy/strategy	Vague reference in strategic plan or research policy	Not mentioned at all
	Institutional policies with regard to the university's role in economic development	Institutional policy	Embedded in strategic plan, research policy, etc.	No formal policies

TABLE C2 Coordination and implementation

		SYSTEMATIC	SPORADIC	WEAK
COORDINATION				
National	Economic development and higher education planning are linked	Formal structures Headed by senior minister	Clusters/forums	Occasional meetings
	Link between universities and national authorities	Specific coordination structures or agencies	Some formal structures but no meaningful coordination	No structures, and political rather than professional networks
	Coordination and consensus building of government agencies involved in higher education	Higher education mainstreamed across government departments	Intermittent interaction with ineffective forums	Higher education issues limited mainly to one ministry or directorate
IMPLEMENTATION				
National	Role of the ministry responsible for higher education	Organised ministry with capacity to make predictable allocations	Spots of capacity with some steering instruments	Weak capacity with unpredictable allocations

		STRONG	WEAK	ABSENT
	Implementation to 'steer' higher education towards development	Instruments such as funding or special projects that incentivise institutions/individuals	Occasional grants for special projects	No particular incentive funding
	Balance/ratio of sources of income for institutions	Government, fees and third stream	Mainly government plus student fees	Mainly government with external funders
	Funding consistency	A stable, transparent public funding mechanism based on criteria agreed upon by all actors involved	Funding allocations somewhat predictable but do not allow for long-term planning nor reward enterprising behaviour	No clear funding or incentives from government
Institutional	Specific units, funding or appointments linked to economic development	Specific units, funding or appointments	Economic development initiatives aspect of a unit or appointment	Mainly ad hoc, staff-initiated operations
	Incentives and rewards for development-related activities	Incentives or counts towards promotion	Some signals but largely rhetoric	No mention
	Teaching programmes linked to the labour market	Targets for enrolments in fields considered to be of high economic relevance	Some programmes in response to specific industry requests	No new programmes linked to labour market
	Special programmes linking students to economic development	Entrepreneurship, work-based learning and/or incubators for students mainstreamed	Ad hoc programmes	No special programmes
	Research activities are becoming more economy-oriented	Research policy/strategy has an economic development focus	Some research agendas have an economic development focus	Ad hoc project funding
	Levels of government and institutional funding for research	High	Medium	Low

Appendix D
Problems in collecting academic core data

Some universities could not extract the required data because they did not have appropriate or functional electronic student and staff data bases. In these cases, the data were only available in the form of summarised tables in print format. Where electronic data bases were in place, the data were often incomplete, classifications were inaccurate, graduate sets were incomplete, and not all marks used to indicate student success in specific courses had been captured.

A number of universities had no central management information office in which complete sets of the data were stored. In these circumstances data had to be collected directly from faculties or administrative departments. A consequence of this decentralisation was that different versions of data on students and staff were held by the university's various operational units. Because the focus of some universities was almost entirely on full-time student enrolments and their full-time staff establishment, their information on part-time students and part-time staff was poor and incomplete. The concepts of full-time equivalent students and full-time equivalent staff were not widely used. The data elements needed to make the necessary calculations were not available in a directly usable format in the case of most of the universities.

Copies of official documents such as annual reports and planning documents were brought back to South Africa and were used to check and correct the data on the CHET templates. Statistical reports found on the internet, as well as on the websites of the universities, were also used to check and correct data. Finally, where inconsistencies or gaps in the data or unusual trends were observed, the data were adjusted on the basis of analyses of average annual growth rates, and average ratios between data elements.

Appendix E

Academic core indicators and ratings

TABLE E1 Academic core indicators measurements and ratings used in the synthesis of the findings from the eight case studies

Indicators	Measurements	Ratings		
		Strong	**Medium**	**Weak**
1 SET enrolments	SET enrolments as % of total enrolments: average for 2001–2007	% of enrolments in SET >39%	% of enrolments in SET between 30% and 39%	% of enrolments in SET <30%
2 Postgraduate enrolments	Masters and doctoral enrolments as % of total enrolments: average for 2001–2007	% of enrolments in masters plus doctors >9%	% of enrolments in masters plus doctors between 5% and 9%	% of enrolments in masters plus doctors <5%
3 Student–staff ratios	FTE academic staff to FTE enrolled student ratios: average for 2001–2007	Student to academic staff ratio <20	Student to academic staff ratio between 20 and 30	Student to academic staff ratio >30
4 Qualifications of academic staff	Proportion of permanent academic staff with doctorates: 2007 only	Permanent academic staff with doctorates >49%	Permanent academic staff with doctorates between 30% and 49%	Permanent academic staff with doctorates <30%
5 Availability of research funding	Research income per permanent academic staff member in purchasing power parity (PPP) dollars: 2007 only	Research funding per academic >PPP$20 000	Research funding per academic between PPP$10 000 and PPP$20 000	Research funding per academic < PPP$10 000
6 SET outputs	SET graduates divided by SET enrolments: average for 2001–2007	Ratio of SET graduates to SET enrolments >20%	Ratio of SET graduates to SET enrolments between 17% and 20%	Ratio of SET graduates to SET enrolments <17%
7 Knowledge production: doctoral graduates	Doctoral graduates as % of permanent academics: average for 2001–2007	Doctoral graduates in given year >10% of total permanent academic staff in that year	Doctoral graduates in given year between 5% and 10% of total permanent academic staff in that year	Doctoral graduates in given year <5% of total permanent academic staff in that year
8 Knowledge production: research publications	Research publications per permanent academic: average for 2001–2007	Ratio of 0.50 of publication units per permanent academic >0.50	Ratio of publication units per permanent academic between 0.25 and 0.50	Ratio of publication units per permanent academic <0.25

Appendix F
Academic core rating descriptions

TABLE F1 Description of academic core ratings used in the analysis of the findings of the eight case studies

Indicators		Strong	Medium	Weak
1	Strong science and technology	SET enrolments growing, and SET share of enrolment shape increasing. Graduation rates of cohorts of SET students minimum of 70%.	SET share of enrolment shape steady. Graduation rate of cohorts of SET students 60% to 70%.	SET enrolments static, and SET share of enrolment shape declining. Graduation rate of cohorts of SET students below 60%.
2	Increased postgraduate enrolments and outputs	Postgraduates at least 25% of total enrolment. Masters and doctoral enrolments and graduates increasing. Ratio of masters to doctoral enrolments no more than 5:1. Ratio of graduates in year to enrolments in same year: masters 25%, doctorates 20%.	Postgraduates as proportion of total enrolments above 10% and increasing. Ratio of masters to doctoral enrolments no more than 10:1. Ratios of graduates to enrolments: masters 20%, doctorates 15%.	Postgraduate enrolments and graduates grow at average annual rate below that of undergraduates. Postgraduates 10% or less of total enrolment. Ratio of masters to doctoral enrolments above 10:1.
3	Teaching loads of academic staff	FTE academic staff ratio close to growth in FTE students. FTE student to academic staff ratios maximum of 15:1 for SET, and maximum average of 20:1 for: all programmes.	FTE students grow at faster rate than FTE academic staff. FTE student to academic staff ratios close 20:1 for SET, close to 30:1 for all programmes.	FTE students grow at faster rate than FTE academic staff ratio. FTE student to academic staff ratios more than 20:1 for SET, and 30:1 for all programmes.
4	Qualifications of academic staff	At least 50% of permanent academic staff have doctorates.	Between 30% and 50% of permanent academic staff have doctorates.	Less than 30% of permanent academic staff have doctorates.
5	Availability of research funding	Annual research funding of greater than PPP$ 20 000 per permanent academic.	Annual research funding of between PPP$ 10 000 and PPP$ 20 000 per permanent academic.	Annual research funding of less than PPP$ 10 000 per permanent academic.
6	Doctoral graduates	Doctoral graduates in given year = 10% or higher of permanent academic staff.	Doctoral graduates in given year between 5% & 9.9% of permanent academic staff.	Doctoral graduates in given year < 5% of permanent academic staff.
7	Research publications	Ratio of 0.50 or higher of publication units per permanent academic.	Ratio of publication units per permanent academic between 0.25 and 0.49.	Ratio of publication units per permanent academic < 0.25.